NEW COLLECTED POEMS
Wendell Berry

NEW COLLECTED POEMS

❀❀❀❀❀❀❀❀❀❀❀❀❀❀❀❀❀

Wendell Berry

COUNTERPOINT

BERKELEY

Library of Congress Cataloging-in-Publication Data is available

ISBN 978-1-61902-152-5

Cover design by Gerilyn Attebery
Interior design by David Bullen

COUNTERPOINT
2560 Ninth Street, Suite 318
Berkeley, CA 94710
www.counterpointpress.com

Printed in the United States of America

12

To Tanya, as before

Contents

OPENINGS (1968)

FARMING: A HAND BOOK (1970)

ix

THE COUNTRY OF MARRIAGE (1973)

CLEARING (1977)

A PART (1980)

THE WHEEL (1982)

ENTRIES (1994)

GIVEN (2005)

LEAVINGS (2010)

The Country of Déjà Vu

My old poems—I liked them all
well enough when they were new.
They came through the air, I wrote them down,
and sent them on, as also I fed
the birds who descended here to eat
as they were passing through. Now
I'm asked to read those poems again.
What for? They all are from the Country
of Déjà Vu, *which is where*
I have no need to go back to.

THE BROKEN GROUND

(1964)

For my mother and father

ELEGY

Pryor Thomas Berry
March 4, 1864 – February 23, 1946

I.

All day our eyes could find no resting place.
Over a flood of snow sight came back
Empty to the mind. The sun
In a shutter of clouds, light
Staggered down the fall of snow.
All circling surfaces of earth were white.
No shape or shadow moved the flight
Of winter birds. Snow held the earth its silence.
We could pick no birdsong from the wind.
At nightfall our father turned his eyes away.
It was this storm of silence shook out his ghost.

2.

We sleep; he only wakes
Who is unshapen in a night of snow.
His shadow in the shadow of the earth
Moves the dark to wholeness.
We wait beside his body here, his image
Shape of silence in the room.

3.

                Sifting
Down the wind, the winter rain
Spirals about the town
And the church hill's jut of stones.
Under the mounds, below

The weather's moving, the numb dead know
No fitfulness of wind.

On the road that in his knowledge ends
We bear our father to the earth.
We have adorned the shuck of him
With flowers as for a bridal, burned
Lamps about him, held death apart
Until the grave should mound it whole.

Behind us rain breaks the corners
Of our father's house, quickens
On the downslope to noise.
       Our steps
Clamor in his silence, who tracked
The sun to autumn in the dust.
         Below the hill
The river bears the rain away, that cut
His fields their shape and stood them dry.

Water wearing the earth
Is the shape of the earth,
The river flattening in its bends.
Their mingling held
Ponderable in his words—
Knowledge polished on a stone.

  4.
River and earth and sun and wind disjoint,
Over his silence flow apart. His words
Are sharp to memory as cold rain
But are not ours.
      We stare dumb
Upon the fulcrum dust, across which death
Lifts up our love. There is no more to add
To this perfection. We turn away
Into the shadow of his death.

Time in blossom and fruit and seed,
Time in the dust huddles in his darkness.
The world, spun in its shadow, holds all.
Until the morning comes his death is ours.

Until morning comes say of the blind bird:
His feet are netted with darkness, or he flies
His heart's distance in the darkness of his eyes.
A season's sun will light him no tree green.

     5.

Spring tangles shadow and light,
Branches of trees
Knit vision and wind.
The shape of the wind is a tree
Bending, spilling its birds.
From the cloud to the stone
The rain stands tall,
Columned into his darkness.
The church hill heals our father in.
Our remembering moves from a different place.

OBSERVANCE

The god of the river leans
against the shore in the early
morning, resting from his caprices;

the gentle sun parades
on his runneled gaze—he devotes
himself to watching it as one
devotes oneself to sleep;
                    the light becomes
his consciousness, warming him.

The river clears after the winter
floods; the slopes of the hills renew
the sun, diaphanous flower and leaf, blue-green
with distance;
                    this idle god dallies
in his shade, his mind adorned with stones.

At the river's edge there is singing;
the townsmen have come down from their sleep,
their singing silences the birds;
they sing renewal beyond irreparable
divisions.
          The god did not expect
these worshippers, but he hears
them singing, briefly as reeds
grown up by the water;
                    they go
away, the river re-enters
their silence
          —and he watches
a white towboat approach, shoving
its rust-colored island of barges,
the sound of its engines filling his mind

and draining out;
                    the forked wake
wrinkles on his vision, pointing
to the corner of his eye,
and floats away;
                    the holiday fishermen
arrive—
          a man and his wife
establish themselves on a sandbar, bringing
lunch in a basket, blankets, tackle
down the path through the young
horseweeds;
                the woman smooths
a blanket on the sand, and begins
a ponderous sunbath, her eyes
covered, her skirt hoisted
above her knees;
                    the man
casts a baited line downstream
and uncaps a beer:
                        the god observes;
these are the sundry
objects of his thought.

He has watched the passing
of other boats, assemblages,
seasons, inundations,
                    boatmen
whose voyages bore down the currents
to the dark shores of their eyes

—and has forgotten them, innocent
of his seasonal wraths, his mischiefs
accomplished and portending, as his present
forbearance is innocent;
                        the perfection

of his forgetting allows the sun
to glitter
               —the light
flows away, its blue and white
peeling off the green waves.

His mind contains
the river as its banks
constrain it, in a single act
receiving it and letting it go.

BOONE

Beyond this final house
I'll make no journeys, that is
the nature of this place,
I came here old; the house contains
the shade of its walls,
a fire in winter; I know
from what direction to expect the wind;
still
    I move in the descent
of days from what was dreamed
to what remains.
In the stillness of this single place
where I'm resigned to die
I'm not free of journeys:
one eye watches while the other sleeps
—every day is a day's remove
from what I knew.

We held a country in our minds
which, unpossessed, allowed
the encroachment of our dreams;
our vision descended like doves
at morning on valleys still blue
in the extremity of hills
until we moved in a prodigy of reckonings,
sustaining in the toil of a journey
the rarity of our desire.

We came there at the end of spring,
climbing out of the hill's shadow
in the evening,
           the light
leaned quiet on the trees,
we'd foreseen no words;
after nightfall when the coals of our fire

contained all that was left
of vision, my journey relinquished me
to sleep;
            kindling in the uneasy
darkness where we
broached our coming to the place we'd dreamed
the dying green of those valleys
began to live.

My passage grew into that country
like a vine, as if remaining
when I'd gone, responsive to the season's
change, boding a continuance of eyes;
not the place or the distance
made it known to me,
but the direction so ardently obeyed,
preserving my advance
on the edge of virgin light,
broken by my shadow's stride;
I wouldn't recognize the way back.

I approach my death, descend
toward the last fact; it is
not so clear to me now as it once seemed;
when I hunted in the new lands
alone, I could foresee
the skeleton hiding with its wound
after the fear and flesh were gone;
                                    now
it may come as a part of sleep.

In winter the river hides its flowing under the ice
—even then it flows,
bearing interminably down; the black crow flies
into the black night;
the bones of the old dead ache for the house fires.

Death is a conjecture of the seed
and the seasons bear it out;
the wild plum achieves its bloom,
perfects the yellow center of each flower,
submits to violence —
extravagance too grievous for praise;
there are no culminations, no
requitals.

      Freed of distances
and dreams, about to die,
the mind turns back to its approaches:
what else have I known?
                    The search
withholds the joy from what is found,
that has been my sorrow;
love is no more than what remains
of itself.
        There are no arrivals.

At the coming of winter
the birds obey the leviathan flock
that moves them south,
a rhythm of the blood that survives the cold
in pursuit of summer;
and the sun, innocent of time
as the blossom is innocent of ripeness,
faithful to solstice, returns —
and the flocks return;
the season recognizes them.

If it were possible now
I'd make myself submissive
to the weather
as an old tree, without retrospect
of winter, blossoming,

grateful for summers hatched from thrushes' eggs
in the speckled thickets
                    —obedient
to darkness,
be innocent of my dying.

❀❀❀❀❀❀❀

GREEN AND WHITE

The wind scruffing it, the bay
is like a field of green grass,

and the white seagulls afloat
in the hackling of the green bay
are like white flowers blooming
in the field,

            for they are white
and come there, and are still
a while, and leave, and leaving
leave no sign they ever were there.

Green is no memorial to white.

There's danger in it. They fly
beyond idea till they come back.

A MAN WALKING AND SINGING

for James Baker Hall

1.

It is no longer necessary to sleep
in order to dream of our destruction.

We take form within our death, the figures
emerging like shadows in fire.

Who is it? speaking to me of death's beauty.

I think it is my own black angel, as near me
as my flesh. I am never divided from his darkness,
his face the black mask of my face. My eyes
live in his black eye-holes. On his black wings
I rise to sing.
      His mouthing presences attend
my singing:
      Die more lightly than live,
they say. Death is more gay.
         There's no argument
against its certainty, at least, they say.

I know they know as surely as I live my death
exists, and has my shape.

2.

But the man so forcefully walking,
say where he goes,
say what he hears and what he sees
and what he knows
to cause him to stride so merrily.

He goes in spring
through the evening street
to buy bread,

green trees leaning
over the sidewalk,
forsythia yellow
beneath the windows,
birds singing
as birds sing
only in spring,

and he sings, his footsteps
beating the measure of his song.

In an open window
a man and a woman
leaning together
at the room's center
embrace and kiss
as if they met
in passing,
the spring wind
lifting the curtain.

His footsteps carry him
past the window,
deeper into his song.

His singing becomes conglomerate
of all he sees,
leaving the street behind him
runged as a ladder
or the staff of a song.

3.

To his death? Yes.

He walks and sings to his death.

And winter will equal spring.

And for the lovers, even
while they kiss, even though
it is spring, the day ends.

But to the sound of his passing
he sings. It is a kind of triumph
that he grieves—thinking
of the white lilacs in bloom,
profuse, fragrant, white
in excess of all seasonal need,

and of the mockingbird's crooked
arrogant notes, hooking him to the sky
as though no flight
or dying could equal him
at his momentary song.

THE COMPANIONS

When he goes out in the morning
and comes back at night
his landlady is there

watching him, leaning
forward in her chair, one hand
holding the curtain back,

simply curious, simply old,
having stashed away her knickknacks
in three commemorative rooms,

stored up a winter's breathing,
forbidden the cold
to come in. She dreams

she's dying in her sleep
and wakes up afraid, to breath in
again her breathed-out breath.

Who will outlast?
She waits for him, faithful
to his arrivals and to the place;

he brings back life to her,
what he salvages of himself daily
from the shut-out air.

They don't speak.
She just observes his homecoming,
lifelike in her chair

as the shell of a wan moth
holding to the lace.

THE ARISTOCRACY

Paradise might have appeared here,
surprising us, a rackle of sublime coordinates
figuring over the trees, surprising us, even
though the look of the place seems not
altogether unexpectant of such an advent,
seems not altogether willing to settle
for something less: the fine light
prepared in the taut statuary of the oaks;
venerable churches of muted brick;
Greek porches presiding at the ends
of approaches; delicate fanlights over doorways
delicate and symmetrical as air, if air
prepared, preened itself for Paradise
to appear, surprisingly, but not very, in this place
—all it needs to *be* Paradise is populace.

(What has appeared, surprisingly, but not very
—stepping out the door, and down the steps,
groping for each next-lower step
with a left foot her expansive exquisitely garmented
paunch has prevented her seeing for thirty-five
years—is a rich, fat, selfish,
ugly, ignorant, old
bitch, airing her cat.)

THE BIRD KILLER

His enemy, the universe, surrounds him nightly with stars
going nowhere over the cold woods that has grown now,
with nightfall, totally dark, the stars deeper in the sky
than darkness; his thoughts go out alone into the winds
of the woods' dark. He sits in the doorway and softly
plays the guitar; his fingers are stiff and heavy
and touch the strings, not dextrously, so that he plays
his own song, no true copy of a tune; sometimes the notes
go away from melody, form singly, and die out,
singly, in the hollow of the instrument, like single small
lights in the dark; his music has this passion,
that he plays as he can play. All day he has walked
in the woods with his gun, ruin of summer, iron-rust,
crumpled bronze, under the bare trees, devouring song. Now
the trees of darkness grow tall and wide; nobody's
silence is in the woods. In the hush of all birds
who love light, he lets go free to die in the broad woods
in the dark the notes of his song.

AN ARCHITECTURE

Like a room, the clear stanza
of birdsong opens among the noises
of motors and breakfasts.

Among the light's beginnings,
lifting broken gray of the night's
end, the bird hastens to his song

as to a place, a room commenced
at the end of sleep. Around
him his singing is entire.

❊❀❊❀❊❀❊❀❊

CANTICLE

for Robert Hazel

What death means is not this—
the spirit, triumphant in the body's fall,
praising its absence, feeding on music.
If life can't justify and explain itself,
death can't justify and explain it.
A creed and a grave never did equal the life
of anything. Yellow flowers sprout in the clefts
of ancient stones at the beginning of April.
The black clothes of the priests are turned
against the frail yellow of sunlight and petal;
they wait in their blackness to earn joy
by dying. They trust that nothing holy is free,
and so their lives are paid. Money slots
in the altar rails make a jukebox of the world,
the mind paying its gnawed coins for the safety of ignorance.

SPARROW

A sparrow is
his hunger organized.
Filled, he flies
before he knows he's going to.
And he dies by the
same movement: filled
with himself, he goes
by the eye-quick
reflex of his flesh
out of sight,
leaving his perfect
absence without a thought.

A MUSIC

I employ the blind mandolin player
in the tunnel of the Métro. I pay him
a coin as hard as his notes,
and maybe he has employed me, and pays me
with his playing to hear him play.

Maybe we're necessary to each other,
and this vacant place has need of us both
—it's vacant, I mean, of dwellers,
is populated by passages and absences.

By some fate or knack he has chosen
to place his music in this cavity
where there's nothing to look at
and blindness costs him nothing.
Nothing was here before he came.

His music goes out among the sounds
of footsteps passing. The tunnel is the resonance
and meaning of what he plays.
It's his music, not the place, I go by.

In this light which is just a fact, like darkness
or the edge or end of what you may be
going toward, he turns his cap up on his knees
and leaves it there to ask and wait, and holds up
his mandolin, the lantern of his world;

his fingers make their pattern on the wires.
This is not the pursuing rhythm
of a blind cane pecking in the sun,
but is a singing in a dark place.

TO GO BY SINGING

He comes along the street, singing,
a rag of a man, with his game foot and bum's clothes.
He's asking for nothing—his hands
aren't even held out. His song
is the gift of singing, to him
and to all who will listen.

To hear him, you'd think the engines
would all stop, and the flower vendor would stand
with her hands full of flowers and not move.
You'd think somebody would have hired him
and provided him a clean quiet stage to sing on.

But there's no special occasion or place
for his singing—that's why it needs
to be strong. His song doesn't impede the morning
or change it, except by freely adding itself.

THE WILD

In the empty lot—a place
not natural, but wild—among
the trash of human absence,

the slough and shamble
of the city's seasons, a few
old locusts bloom.

A few woods birds
fly and sing
in the new foliage

—warblers and tanagers, birds
wild as leaves; in a million
each one would be rare,

new to the eyes. A man
couldn't make a habit
of such color,

such flight and singing.
But they're the habit of this
wasted place. In them

the ground is wise. They are
its remembrance of what it is.

MAY SONG

For whatever is let go
there's a taker.
The living discovers itself

where no preparation
was made for it,
where its only privilege

is to live if it can.
The window flies from the dark
of the subway mouth

into the sunlight
stained with the green
of the spring weeds

that crowd the improbable
black earth
of the embankment,

their stout leaves
like the tongues and bodies
of a herd, feeding

on the new heat,
drinking at the seepage
of the stones:

the freehold of life,
triumphant
even in the waste

of those who possess it.
But it is itself the possessor,
we know at last,

seeing it send out weeds
to take back
whatever is left:

Proprietor, pasturing foliage
on the rubble,
making use

of the useless—a beauty
we have less than not
deserved.

❀❀❀❀❀❀❀

THE FEAR OF DARKNESS

The tall marigolds darken.
The baby cries
for better reasons than it knows.
The young wife walks
and walks among the shadows
meshed in the rooms.
And he sits in the doorway,
looking toward the woods,
long after the stars come out.
He feels the slow
sky turn toward him, and wait.
His birthright
is a third-hand Chevrolet,
bought for too much. "I
floorboard the son of a bitch,
and let her go."

THE PLAN

My old friend, the owner
of a new boat, stops by
to ask me to fish with him,

and I say I will — both of us
knowing that we may never
get around to it, it may be

years before we're both
idle again on the same day.
But we make a plan, anyhow,

in honor of friendship
and the fine spring weather
and the new boat

and our sudden thought
of the water shining
under the morning fog.

THE GUEST

Washed into the doorway
by the wake of the traffic,
he wears humanity
like a third-hand shirt
—blackened with enough
of Manhattan's dirt to sprout
a tree, or poison one.
His empty hand has led him
where he has come to.
Our differences claim us.
He holds out his hand,
in need of all that's mine.

And so we're joined, as deep
as son and father. His life
is offered me to choose.

*Shall I begin servitude
to him? Let this cup pass.
Who am I?* But charity must
suppose, knowing no better,
that this is a man fallen
among thieves, or come
to this strait by no fault
—that our difference
is not a judgment,
though I can afford to eat
and am made his judge.

I am, I nearly believe,
the Samaritan who fell
into the ambush of his heart
on the way to another place.
My stranger waits, his hand

held out like something to read,
as though its emptiness
is an accomplishment.
I give him a smoke and the price
of a meal, no more

—not sufficient kindness
or believable sham.
I paid him to remain strange
to my threshold and table,
to permit me to forget him—
knowing I won't. He's the guest
of my knowing, though not asked.

❀❀❀❀❀❀

THE THIEF

I think of us lying asleep,
eyes and hands filled with the dark,
when the arm of the night
entered, reaching into the pockets
of our empty clothes. We slept
in the element of that power,
innocent of it, preserved from it
not even by our wish.
As though not born, we were carried
beyond an imminence we did not
waken to, as passively as stars
are carried beyond their spent
shining—our eyes granted to the light
again, by what chance or price
we do not even know.

THE BROKEN GROUND

The opening out and out,
body yielding body:
the breaking
through which the new
comes, perching
above its shadow
on the piling up
darkened broken old
husks of itself:
bud opening to flower
opening to fruit opening
to the sweet marrow
of the seed —
          taken
from what was, from
what could have been.
What is left
is what is.

FINDINGS

(1969)

THE DESIGN OF THE HOUSE:
IDEAL AND HARD TIME

1.

Except in idea, perfection is as wild
as light; there is no hand laid on it.
But the house is a shambles
unless the vision of its perfection
upholds it like stone.

More probable: the ideal
of its destruction:
cloud of fire prefiguring
its disappearance.

What value there is
is assumed;
like a god, the house elects its omens;
because it is, I desire it should be
—white, its life intact in it,
among trees.

Love has conceived a house,
and out of its labor
brought forth its likeness
—the emblem of desire, continuing
though the flesh falls away.

2.

We've come round again
to short days and long nights;
time goes;

the clocks barely keep up;
a spare dream of summer
          is kept
alive in the house:

the Queen Anne's lace
          —gobletted,
green beginning to bloom,
tufted, upfurling—
unfolding
          whiteness:

in this winter's memory
more clear than ever in summer,
cold paring away excess:

the single blooming random
in the summer's abundance
of its kind, in high relief
above the clover and grass
of the field, unstill
          an instant,
the day having come upon it,
          green and white
in as much light as ever was.

Opened, white, at the solstice
of its becoming, then the flower
forgets its growing;
          is still;

dirt is its paradigm—
and this memory's seeing,
a cold wind keening the outline.

3.

Winter nights the house sleeps,
a dry seedhead in the snow
falling and fallen, the white
and dark and depth of it, continuing
slow impact of silence.
                    The dark
rooms hold our heads on pillows, waiting
day, through the snow falling and fallen
in the darkness between inconsecutive
dreams. The brain burrows in its earth
and sleeps,
                    trusting dawn, though the sun's
light is a light without precedent, never
proved ahead of its coming, waited for
by the law that hope has made it.

4.

What do you intend?
                    Drink blood
and speak, old ghosts. I don't
hear you. What has it amounted to
—the unnegotiable accumulation
of your tears? Your expenditure
has purchased no reprieve. Your
failed wisdom shards among the
down-going atoms of the moment.

History goes blind and in darkness;
neither sees nor is seen, nor is
known except as a carrion
marked with unintelligible wounds:
dragging its dead body, living,
yet to be born, it moves heavily
to its glories. It tramples
the little towns, forgets their names.

5.

If reason were all, reason
would not exist—the will
to reason accounts for it;
it's not reason that chooses
to live; the seed doesn't swell
in its husk by reason, but loves
itself, obeys light which is
its own thought and argues the leaf
in secret; love articulates
the choice of life in fact; life
chooses life because it is
alive; what lives didn't begin dead,
nor sun's fire commence in ember.

Love foresees a jointure
composing a house, a marriage
of contraries, compendium
of opposites in equilibrium.
This morning the sun
came up before the moon set;
shadows were stripped from the house
like burnt rags, the sky turning
blue behind the clear moon,
day and night moving to day.

Let severances be as dividing
budleaves around the flower
—woman and child enfolded, chosen.
It's a dying begun, not lightly,
the taking up of this love
whose legacy is its death.

6.

This is a love poem for you, Tanya —

among wars, among the brutal forfeitures
of time, in this house, among its latent fires,
among all that honesty must see, I accept
your dying, and love you: nothing mitigates
—and for our Mary, chosen by the blind
hungering of our blood, precious and periled
in her happy mornings; whose tears are mine.

7.

There's still a degree of sleep
          recalls
the vast empty dream I slept in
          as a child
sometimes contained a chaos, tangled
like fishline snarled in hooks —
sometimes a hook, whetted, severe,
          drawing
the barbed darkness to a point;
sometimes I seemed merely to be falling.

The house, also, has taken shape in it.

8.

And I have dreamed
of the morning coming in
like a bird through the window
not burdened by a thought,

the light a singing
as I hoped.

It comes in and sings
on the corner of the white washstand,

among coleus stems and roots
in a clear green bottle
on the black tabletop
beneath the window,

under the purple coleus leaves,

among spearing
green philodendron leaves,
on the white washstand:

a small yellow bird with black wings,
darting in and out.

9.

To imagine the thoughtlessness
of a thoughtless thing
is useless.
The mind must sing
of itself to keep awake.

Love has visualized a house,
and out of its expenditure
fleshed the design
at this cross ways
of consciousness and time:

its form is growth
come to light in it;

croplands, gardens,
are of its architecture,

labor its realization;

solstice is the height
of its consciousness,

thicket a figuration
of its waking;

plants and stars are made convergent
in its windows;

cities we have gone to and come back
are the prospect of its doorways.

And there's a city it dreams of:
salt-white beside the water.

10.

Waking comes into sleep like a dream:
violet dawn over the snow, the black trees.

Snow and the house's white make a white
the black swifts may come back to.

THE HANDING DOWN

1. *The light*

The mind is the continuity
of its objects, and the coherence
of its objects—the

understanding of each
one thing by the
intelligence of an assemblage.

It is the effort of design
to triumph over the imperfections
of the parts—

the old man's gathering of memories
toward this morning's windows
and pipe and talk, the road

and housefronts all his years
have come by, the squash blooms
of this summer's garden.

The mind falsifies its objects
by inattention. Indirection
is its debasement of what it loves.

It is not given proof
that it is true. It is blind
at the beginning and at the end.

It is the illumination of a passage,
no more.

2. *The conversation*

Speaker and hearer, words
making a passage between them,
begin a community.
                              Two minds

in succession, grandfather
and grandson, they sit and talk
on the enclosed porch,

looking out at the town, which
recalls itself in their talk
and is carried forward.

Their conversation has
no pattern of its own,
but alludes casually

to a shaped knowledge
in the minds of the two men
who love each other.

The quietness of knowing in common
is half of it. Silences come into it
easily, and break it

while the old man thinks
or concentrates on his pipe
and the strong smoke

climbs over the brim of his hat.
He has lived a long time.
He has seen the changes of times

and grown used to the world
again. Having been wakeful so long,
the loser of so many years,

his mind moves back and forth,
sorting and counting,
among all he knows.

His memory has become huge,
and surrounds him,
and fills his silences.

He lifts his head
and speaks of an old day
that amuses him or grieves him

or both.
Under the windows opposite them
there's a long table loaded

with potted plants, the foliage
staining and shadowing the daylight
as it comes in.

3. *The old man is older in history than in time*
"I've lived in two countries
in my life
and never moved."

He has spoken of the steamboats
of his boyhood, the whistles
still clear to him

in the upriver bends,
coming down to the landings
now disappeared, their names

less spoken every year.
He has remembered the open days
of that first country

—"It was *free* here
when I was a boy"—and the old
brutalities and sorrows.

And now they talk of power
and politics and war, agonies
now, and to come,

deaths never imagined
by the old man's generation.
The mistakes of the old

become the terrors of the young.
In the face of his grandson he sees
something of himself, going on.

Moved by the near suffering
of other men, he has taken them
into the body of his thought.

"If I died now, I wouldn't lose
much. It's you young ones
I worry about."

    4. *He looks out the window at the town*
Beyond the windows, past the fern
and the pot rims and the patterned
vine leaves, and the trees

in the yard, are the white housefronts
and storefronts of the little town,
facing the road. There are only

the two directions: coming in
and going out. And all
who take one take both.

The town, "port of entry
and departure for the bodies
as well as the souls of men,"

aspires to the greatness of the greatest
city of the mind—with its dead
for baggage. It suffers its dead beside it

under the particular grass, the summary stone.
Their hill keeps a silence into which
the live town speaks a little.

They are the town's shut record, all
their complexity perished—victims
of epidemics, meanness, foolishness,

heredity, war, recklessness, chance,
pride, time. None ever escaped.
That is the history of the place.

The town, its white walls
gleaming among black
shadows and green leaves,

stands on the surface of the eye.
And the town's history is the eye's
depth and recognition—is the mind's

discovery of itself in its place
in a new morning.

5. *He has lived through another night*
He begins the knowledge
of the sun's absence.
He's likely to wake up

any hour of the night
out of his light sleep
to know—with clarity like

the touch of hands in the dark—
the stillness of the room.
The silence

stretches over the town
like a black tent, whose hem
the headstones weight.

Into it come, now
and again, hard footsteps
on the road, remote

sudden voices, and then
a car coming in, or
going out, the headlights

levering the window's
image around the walls.

                    +

And he considers the size
of his life, lying in it there,
looking up out of it

into the darkness,

the transparence of all
his old years between him
and the darkness.

                +

Before it's light
the birds waken, and begin
singing in the dark trees

around the house, among the leaves
over the dampened roofs
of the still town

and in the country thickets
for miles. Their voices
reach to the end of the dark.

6. *The new house*

At the foot of his long shadow
he walked across the town
early in the morning

to watch the carpenters at work
on a new house. The saws released
the warm pine-smell into the air

—the scent of time to come, freshly
opened. He was comforted by that,
and by the new unblemished wood.

That time goes, making
the jointures of households, for better
or worse, is no comfort.

That, for the men and women
still to be born, time is coming
is a comfort of sorts.

That there's a little of the good
left over from a few lives
is a comfort of sorts.

He has grown eager
in his love for the good dead
and all the unborn.

That failed hope
doesn't prove the failure of hope
is a comfort of sorts.

Grown old and wise, he takes
what comfort he can get, as gladly as once
he'd have taken the comfort he wished for.

For a man knowing evil—how surely
it grows up in any ground and makes seed—
the building of a house is a craft indeed.

7. *The heaviness of his wisdom*
The incredible happens, he knows.
The worst possibilities are real.
The terrible justifies

his dread of it. He knows winter
despondences, the mind inundated
by its excrement, hope gone

and not remembered.
And he knows vernal transfigurations,
the sentence in the stems of trees

noisy with old memory made new,
troubled with the seed
of the being of what has not been.

He trusts the changes of the sun and air:
dung and carrion made earth,
richness that forgets what it was.

He knows, if he can hold out
long enough, the good
is given its chance.

He has dreamed of a town
fit for the abiding of souls
and bodies that might live forever.

He has seen it as in a far-off
white and gold evening
of summer, the black flight

of swifts turning above it
in the air. There's a clarity
in which he has not become clear,

his body dragging a shadow,
half hidden in it.

    8. *A wilderness starts toward him*

The old man lives on
among sheds and tools
he won't use again, places

he won't go back to.
Around the place his living
has kept clear there's a wilderness

waiting for him to go.
In the wooded creek vales
of his memory, that his mind

opens slowly to become, all is
as it was, and must be,
the water thrush's note chinks

like dropping water
over the rocks. To old fields
and croplands the persistent

anachronism of wilderness
returns, oaks deepen in the hill,
their branches mesh,

into the pocketed shadows
slowly as rocks wear
the moss comes.

Behind him, as if imagined
before his birth, he leaves
silence no one has yet broken.

Ahead of him he sees, as in an old
forefather's prophetic dream,
the woods take back the land.

9. *Though he can't know death, he must study dying*
Knowing he must learn to die
or be beaten, he has looked
toward what he must come to,

that bad exchange
of all he knows for all
he doesn't.

He has become the sufferer
of what he cannot help.
Knowing the euphemisms

of the salesmen leave the mind
wordless before its trials,
he has learned

among the quick plants
of his memory
to speak of their end.

When vision is marketed to win
there's nothing in victory to desire.
And it's not victory

that he's going toward.
He leaves that for the others,
the younger, who will leave it.

It's a vision that generous men
make themselves willing to give up
in order to have.

His luxury is the giving up of vanity:
"Why should a man eighty-one years old
care how he looks?"

10. *The freedom of loving*

After his long wakeful life,
he has come to love the world
as though it's not to be lost.

Though he faces darkness, his hands
have no weight or harshness
on his small granddaughters' heads.

His love doesn't ask that they understand
it includes them. It includes, as freely,
the green plant leaves in the window,

clusters of white ripe peaches weighting
the branch among the weightless leaves.
There was an agony in ripening

that becomes irrelevant at last
to ripeness. His love
turned away from death, freely,

is equal to it.

   11. *He takes his time*
There's no need to hurry
to die. His days are received
and let go, as birds fly

through the broken windows
of an old house. All his traps
are baited, but not set.

On the porch, in the potato rows,
among the shades and neighbors
of his summer walks,

he finds time
for the perfecting of gifts.

   12. *The fern*
His intimate the green fern
lives in his eye, its profusion
veiling the earthen pot,

the leaves lighted and shadowed
among the actions of the morning.
Between the fern and the old man

there has been conversation
all their lives. The leaves
have spoken to his eyes.

He has replied with his hands.
In his handing it has come down
Until now—a living

that has survived
all successions and sheddings.
Even when he was a boy

plants were his talent. His mother
would give him the weak ones
until he made them grow,

then buy them, healed, for dimes.
And from her he inherits
the fern, the life of it

on which the new leaves crest.
It feeds on the sun and the dirt
and does not hasten.

It has forgotten all deaths.

13. *He is in the habit of the world*
The world has finally worn him
until he is no longer strange to it.
His face has grown comfortable on him.

His hat is shaped to his way
of putting it on and taking it off,
the crown bordered

with the dark graph of his sweat.
He has become a scholar of plants
and gardens, the student

of his memory, attentive to pipesmoke
and the movements of shadows. His days
come to him as if they know him.

He has become one of the familiars
of the place, like a landmark
the birds no longer fear.

Among the greens of full summer,
among shadows like monuments,
he makes his way down,

loving the earth he will become.

14. *The young man, thinking of the old*
While we talk we hear across the town
two hammers galloping on a roof, and the high
curving squeal of an electric saw.

That is happening deep in the town's being,
as weighted and clumsy with its hope
as a pregnant woman or a loaded barge.

And the old man sitting beside me knows
the tools and vision of a builder
of houses, and the uses of those.

His strong marriage has made
the accuracy of his dwelling.
As though always speaking openly

in a clear room, he has made
the ways of neighborhood
between his house and the town.

His life has been a monument to the place.
His garden rows go back through all
his summers, bearing their fading

script of vine and bloom,
what he has written on the ground,
its kind abundance, taken kindly from it.

Now, resting from his walk,
he's comforted by the sounds
of hammering, half listened to.

He is comforted, not because he hopes
for much, but because he knows
of hope, its losses and uses.

He has gone in the world, visioning
a house worthy of the child
newborn in it.

THREE ELEGIAC POEMS

Harry Erdman Perry, 1881–1965

I

Let him escape hospital and doctor,
    the manners and odors of strange places,
    the dispassionate skills of experts.

Let him go free of tubes and needles,
    public corridors, the surgical white
    of life dwindled to poor pain.

Foreseeing the possibility of life without
    possibility of joy, let him give it up.

Let him die in one of the old rooms
    of his living, no stranger near him.

Let him go in peace out of the bodies
    of his life —
    flesh and marriage and household.

From the wide vision of his own windows
    let him go out of sight; and the final

time and light of his life's place be
    last seen before his eyes' slow
    opening in the earth.

Let him go like one familiar with the way
    into the wooded and tracked and
    furrowed hill, his body.

II

I stand at the cistern in front of the old barn
in the darkness, in the dead of winter,

the night strangely warm, the wind blowing,
rattling an unlatched door.
I draw the cold water up out of the ground, and drink.

At the house the light is still waiting.
An old man I have loved all my life is dying
in his bed there. He is going
slowly down from himself.
In final obedience to his life, he follows
his body out of our knowing.
Only his hands, quiet on the sheet, keep
a painful resemblance to what they no longer are.

III

He goes free of the earth.
The sun of his last day sets
clear in the sweetness of his liberty.

The earth recovers from his dying,
the hallow of his life remaining
in all his death leaves.

Radiances know him. Grown lighter
than breath, he is set free
in our remembering. Grown brighter

than vision, he goes dark
into the life of the hill
that holds his peace.

He is hidden among all that is,
and cannot be lost.

OPENINGS

(1968)

THE THOUGHT OF SOMETHING ELSE

1.

A spring wind blowing
the smell of the ground
through the intersections of traffic,
the mind turns, seeks a new
nativity—another place,
simpler, less weighted
by what has already been.

Another place!
it's enough to grieve me—
that old dream of going,
of becoming a better man
just by getting up and going
to a better place.

2.

The mystery. The old
unaccountable unfolding.
The iron trees in the park
suddenly remember forests.
It becomes possible to think of going.

3.

—a place where thought
can take its shape
as quietly in the mind
as water in a pitcher,

or a man can be
safely without thought
— see the day begin
and lean back,
a simple wakefulness filling
perfectly
the spaces among the leaves.

MY GREAT-GRANDFATHER'S SLAVES

Deep in the back ways of my mind I see them
   going in the long days
   over the same fields that I have gone
   long days over.

I see the sun passing and burning high
   over that land from their day
   until mine, their shadows
   having risen and consumed them.

I see them obeying and watching
   the bearded tall man whose voice
   and blood are mine, whose countenance
   in stone at his grave my own resembles,
   whose blindness is my brand.

I see them kneel and pray to the white God
   who buys their souls with Heaven.

I see them approach, quiet
   in the merchandise of their flesh,
   to put down their burdens
   of firewood and hemp and tobacco
   into the minds of my kinsmen.

I see them moving in the rooms of my history,
   the day of my birth entering
   the horizon emptied of their days,
   their purchased lives taken back
   into the dust of birthright.

I see them borne, shadow within shadow,
   shroud within shroud, through all nights
   from their lives to mine, long beyond

reparation or given liberty
or any straightness.

I see them go in the bonds of my blood
through all the time of their bodies.

I have seen that freedom cannot be taken
from one man and given to another,
and cannot be taken and kept.

I know that freedom can only be given,
and is the gift to the giver
from the one who receives.

I am owned by the blood of all of them
who ever were owned by my blood.
We cannot be free of each other.

OCTOBER 10

Now constantly there is the sound,
quieter than rain,
of the leaves falling.

Under their loosening bright
gold, the sycamore limbs
bleach whiter.

Now the only flowers
are beeweed and aster, spray
of their white and lavender
over the brown leaves.

The calling of a crow sounds
loud—a landmark—now
that the life of summer falls
silent, and the nights grow.

THE SNAKE

At the end of October
I found on the floor of the woods
a small snake whose back
was patterned with the dark
of the dead leaves he lay on.
His body was thickened with a mouse
or small bird. He was cold,
so stuporous with his full belly
and the fall air that he hardly
troubled to flicker his tongue.
I held him a long time, thinking
of the perfection of the dark
marking on his back, the death
that swelled him, his living cold.
Now the cold of him stays
in my hand, and I think of him
lying below the frost,
big with a death to nourish him
during a long sleep.

THE COLD

How exactly good it is
to know myself
in the solitude of winter,

my body containing its own
warmth, divided from all
by the cold; and to go

separate and sure
among the trees cleanly
divided, thinking of you

perfect too in your solitude,
your life withdrawn into
your own keeping

—to be clear, poised
in perfect self-suspension
toward you, as though frozen.

And having known fully the
goodness of that, it will be
good also to melt.

TO MY CHILDREN, FEARING FOR THEM

Terrors are to come. The earth
is poisoned with narrow lives.
I think of you. What you will

live through, or perish by, eats
at my heart. What have I done? I
need better answers than there are

to the pain of coming to see
what was done in blindness,
loving what I cannot save. Nor,

your eyes turning toward me,
can I wish your lives unmade
though the pain of them is on me.

THE WINTER RAIN

The leveling of the water, its increase,
the gathering of many into much:

in the cold dusk I stop
midway of the creek, listening
as it passes downward
loud over the rocks, under
the sound of the rain striking,
nowhere any sound
but the water, the dead
weedstems soaked with it, the
ground soaked, the earth overflowing.

And having waded all the way
across, I look back and see there
on the water the still sky.

MARCH SNOW

The morning lights
whiteness that has touched the world
perfectly as air.
In the whitened country
under the still fall of the snow
only the river, like a brown earth,
taking all falling darkly
into itself, moves.

❀❀❀❀❀❀❀

APRIL WOODS: MORNING

Birth of color
out of night and the ground.

Luminous the gatherings
of bloodroot

newly risen, green leaf,
white flower

in the sun, the dark
grown absent.

THE FINCHES

The ears stung with cold
sun and frost of dawn
in early April, comes

the song of winter finches,
their crimson bright, then
dark as they move into

and then against the light.
May the year warm them
soon. May they soon go

north with their singing
and the season follow.
May the bare sticks soon

live, and our minds go free
of the ground
into the shining of trees.

THE PORCH OVER THE RIVER

In the dusk of the river, the wind
gone, the trees grow still —
the beautiful poise of lightness,
the heavy world pushing toward it.

Beyond, on the face of the water,
lies the reflection of another tree,
inverted, pulsing with the short strokes
of waves the wind has stopped driving.

In a time when men no longer
can imagine the lives of their sons
this is still the world —
the world of my time, the grind

of engines marking the country
like an audible map, the high dark
marked by the flight of men,
lights stranger than stars.

The phoebes cross and re-cross
the openings, alert
for what may still be earned
from the light. The whippoorwills

begin, and the frogs. And the dark
falls, again, as it must.
The look of the world withdraws
into the vein of memory.

The mirrored tree, darkening, stirs
with the water's inward life. What has
made it so? — a quietness in it
no question can be asked in.

BEFORE DARK

From the porch at dusk I watched
a kingfisher wild in flight
he could only have made for joy.

He came down the river, splashing
against the water's dimming face
like a skipped rock, passing

on down out of sight. And still
I could hear the splashes
farther and farther away

as it grew darker. He came back
the same way, dusky as his shadow,
sudden beyond the willows.

The splashes went on out of hearing.
It was dark then. Somewhere
the night had accommodated him

—at the place he was headed for
or where, led by his delight,
he came.

THE DREAM

I dream an inescapable dream
in which I take away from the country
the bridges and roads, the fences, the strung wires,
ourselves, all we have built and dug and hollowed out,
our flocks and herds, our droves of machines.

I restore then the wide-branching trees.
I see growing over the land and shading it
the great trunks and crowns of the first forest.
I am aware of the rattling of their branches,
the lichened channels of their bark, the saps
of the ground flowing upward to their darkness.
Like the afterimage of a light that only by not
looking can be seen, I glimpse the country as it was.
All its beings belong wholly to it. They flourish
in dying as in being born. It is the life of its deaths.

I must end, always, by replacing
our beginning there, ourselves and our blades,
the flowing in of history, putting back what I took away,
trying always with the same pain of foreknowledge
to build all that we have built, but destroy nothing.

My hands weakening, I feel on all sides blindness
growing in the land on its peering bulbous stalks.
I see that my mind is not good enough.
I see that I am eager to own the earth and to own men.
I find in my mouth a bitter taste of money,
a gaping syllable I can neither swallow nor spit out.
I see all that we have ruined in order to have, all
that was owned for a lifetime to be destroyed forever.

Where are the sleeps that escape such dreams?

THE SYCAMORE

for Harry Caudill

In the place that is my own place, whose earth
I am shaped in and must bear, there is an old tree growing,
a great sycamore that is a wondrous healer of itself.
Fences have been tied to it, nails driven into it,
hacks and whittles cut in it, the lightning has burned it.
There is no year it has flourished in
that has not harmed it. There is a hollow in it
that is its death, though its living brims whitely
at the lip of the darkness and flows outward.
Over all its scars has come the seamless white
of the bark. It bears the gnarls of its history
healed over. It has risen to a strange perfection
in the warp and bending of its long growth.
It has gathered all accidents into its purpose.
It has become the intention and radiance of its dark fate.
It is a fact, sublime, mystical and unassailable.
In all the country there is no other like it.
I recognize in it a principle, an indwelling
the same as itself, and greater, that I would be ruled by.
I see that it stands in its place, and feeds upon it,
and is fed upon, and is native, and maker.

THE MEADOW

In the town's graveyard the oldest plot now frees itself
of sorrow, the myrtle of the graves grown wild. The last
who knew the faces who had these names are dead,
and now the names fade, dumb on the stones, wild
as shadows in the grass, clear to the rabbit and the wren.
Ungrieved, the town's ancestry fits the earth. They become
a meadow, their alien marble grown native as maple.

AGAINST THE WAR IN VIETNAM

Believe the automatic righteousness
of whoever holds an office. Believe
the officials who see without doubt
that peace is assured by war, freedom
by oppression. The truth preserved by lying
becomes a lie. Believe or die.

In the name of ourselves we ride
at the wheels of our engines,
in the name of Plenty devouring all,
the exhaust of our progress falling
deadly on villages and fields
we do not see. We are prepared
for millions of little deaths.

Where are the quiet plenteous dwellings
we were coming to, the neighborly holdings?
We see the American freedom defended
with lies, and the lies defended
with blood, the vision of Jefferson
served by the agony of children,
women cowering in holes.

DARK WITH POWER

Dark with power, we remain
the invaders of our land, leaving
deserts where forests were,
scars where there were hills.

On the mountains, on the rivers,
on the cities, on the farmlands
we lay weighted hands, our breath
potent with the death of all things.

Pray to us, farmers and villagers
of Vietnam. Pray to us, mothers
and children of helpless countries.
Ask for nothing.

We are carried in the belly
of what we have become
toward the shambles of our triumph,
far from the quiet houses.

Fed with dying, we gaze
on our might's monuments of fire.
The world dangles from us
while we gaze.

IN MEMORY: STUART EGNAL

A high wooded hill near Florence, an April
afternoon. Below, the valley farms
were still and small, stall and field
hushed in brightness. Around us the woods
woke with sound, and shadows lived
in the air and on the dry leaves. You
were drawing what we saw. Its forms
and lights reached slowly to your page.
We talked, and laughed at what we said.

Fine hours. The sort men dream
of having, and of having had. Today
while I slept I saw it all
again, and words for you came to me
as though we sat there talking still
in the quick of April. A wakening
strangeness—here in another valley
you never lived to come to—half
a dialogue, keeping on.

THE WANT OF PEACE

All goes back to the earth,
and so I do not desire
pride of excess or power,
but the contentments made
by men who have had little:
the fisherman's silence
receiving the river's grace,
the gardner's musing on rows.

I lack the peace of simple things.
I am never wholly in place.
I find no peace or grace.
We sell the world to buy fire,
our way lighted by burning men,
and that has bent my mind
and made me think of darkness
and wish for the dumb life of roots.

THE PEACE OF WILD THINGS

When despair for the world grows in me
and I wake in the night at the least sound
in fear of what my life and my children's lives may be,
I go and lie down where the wood drake
rests in his beauty on the water, and the great heron feeds.
I come into the peace of wild things
who do not tax their lives with forethought
of grief. I come into the presence of still water.
And I feel above me the day-blind stars
waiting with their light. For a time
I rest in the grace of the world, and am free.

❀❁❀❁❀❁❀❁❀❁

GRACE

for Gurney Norman, quoting him

The woods is shining this morning.
Red, gold and green, the leaves
lie on the ground, or fall,
or hang full of light in the air still.
Perfect in its rise and in its fall, it takes
the place it has been coming to forever.
It has not hastened here, or lagged.
See how surely it has sought itself,
its roots passing lordly through the earth.
See how without confusion it is
all that it is, and how flawless
its grace is. Running or walking, the way
is the same. Be still. Be still.
"He moves your bones, and the way is clear."

TO THINK OF THE LIFE OF A MAN

In a time that breaks
in cutting pieces all around,
when men, voiceless
against thing-ridden men,
set themselves on fire, it seems
too difficult and rare
to think of the life of a man
grown whole in the world,
at peace and in place.
But having thought of it
I am beyond the time
I might have sold my hands
or sold my voice and mind
to the arguments of power
that go blind against
what they would destroy.

MARRIAGE

to Tanya

How hard it is for me, who live
in the excitement of women
and have the desire for them
in my mouth like salt. Yet
you have taken me and quieted me.
You have been such light to me
that other women have been
your shadows. You come near me
with the nearness of sleep.
And yet I am not quiet.
It is to be broken. It is to be
torn open. It is not to be
reached and come to rest in
ever. I turn against you,
I break from you, I turn to you.
We hurt, and are hurt,
and have each other for healing.
It is healing. It is never whole.

DO NOT BE ASHAMED

You will be walking some night
in the comfortable dark of your yard
and suddenly a great light will shine
round about you, and behind you
will be a wall you never saw before.
It will be clear to you suddenly
that you were about to escape,
and that you are guilty: you misread
the complex instructions, you are not
a member, you lost your card
or never had one. And you will know
that they have been there all along,
their eyes on your letters and books,
their hands in your pockets,
their ears wired to your bed.
Though you have done nothing shameful,
they will want you to be ashamed.
They will want you to kneel and weep
and say you should have been like them.
And once you say you are ashamed,
reading the page they hold out to you,
then such light as you have made
in your history will leave you.
They will no longer need to pursue you.
You will pursue them, begging forgiveness.
They will not forgive you.
There is no power against them.
It is only candor that is aloof from them,
only an inward clarity, unashamed,
that they cannot reach. Be ready.
When their light has picked you out
and their questions are asked, say to them:
"I am not ashamed." A sure horizon
will come around you. The heron will begin
his evening flight from the hilltop.

WINDOW POEMS

Window. Window.
The wind's eye
to see into the wind.
The eye in its hollow
looking out
through the black frame
at the waves the wind
drives up the river,
whitecaps, a wild day,
the white sky
traveled by snow squalls,
the trees thrashing,
the corn blades driven,
quivering, straight out.

2.

The foliage has dropped
below the window's grave edge,
baring the sky, the distant
hills, the branches,
the year's greenness
gone down from the high
light where it so fairly
defied falling.
The country opens to the sky,
the eye purified among hard facts:
the black grid of the window,
the wood of trees branching
outward and outward
to the nervousness of twigs,
buds asleep in the air.

3.

The window has forty
panes, forty clarities
variously wrinkled, streaked
with dried rain, smudged,
dusted. The frame
is a black grid
beyond which the world
flings up the wild
graph of its growth,
tree branch, river,
slope of land,
the river passing
downward, the clouds blowing,
usually, from the west,
the opposite way.
The window is a form
of consciousness, pattern
of formed sense
through which to look
into the wild
that is a pattern too,
but dark and flowing,
bearing along the little
shapes of the mind
as the river bears
a sash of some blinded house.
This windy day
on one of the panes
a blown seed, caught
in cobweb, beats and beats.

4.

This is the wind's eye,
Wendell's window
dedicated to purposes

dark to him, a seeing into
days to come, the winds
of the days as they approach
and go by. He has come
mornings of four years
to be thoughtful here
while day and night
cold and heat
beat upon the world.
In the low room
within the weathers,
sitting at the window,
he has shed himself
at times, and been renewed.
The spark at his wrist
flickers and dies, flickers
and dies. The life in him
grows and subsides
and grows again
like the icicle throbbing
winter after winter
at a wrinkle in the eave,
flowing over itself
as it comes and goes,
fluid as a branch.

5.

Look in
and see him looking out.
He is not always
quiet, but there have been times
when happiness has come
to him, unasked,
like the stillness on the water
that holds the evening clear
while it subsides

—and he let go
what he was not.
His ancestor is the hill
that rises in the winter wind
beyond the blind wall
at his back.
It wears a patched robe
of some history that he knows
and some that he
does not: healed fields
where the woods come back
after a time of crops,
human history
done with, a few
ragged fences surviving
among the trees;
and on the ridges still
there are open fields
where the cattle look up
to watch him on his walks
with eyes patient as time.
The hill has known
too many days and men
grown quiet behind him.
But there are mornings
when his soul emerges
from darkness
as out of a hollow in a tree
high on the crest
and takes flight
with savage joy and harsh
outcry down the long slope
of the leaves. And nights
when he sleeps sweating
under the burden of the hill.
At the window

he sits and looks out,
musing on the river,
a little brown hen duck
paddling upstream
among the windwaves
close to the far bank.
What he has understood
lies behind him
like a road in the woods. He is
a wilderness looking out
at the wild.

6.

A warm day in December,
and the rain falling
steadily through the morning
as the man works
at his table, the window
staring into the valley
as though conscious
when he is not. The cold river
steams in the warm air.
It is rising. Already
the lowest willows
stand in the water
and the swift currents
fold round them.
The bare twigs of the elms
are beaded with bright drops
that grow slowly heavy
and fall, bigger
and slower than the rain.
A fox squirrel comes
through the trees, hurrying
someplace, but it seems
to be raining everywhere,

and he submits to wetness
and sits still, miserable
maybe, for an hour.
How sheltering and clear
the window seems, the dry fireheat
inside, and outside the gray
downpour. As the man works
the weather moves
upon his mind, its dreariness
a kind of comfort.

7.

Outside the window
is a roofed wooden tray
he fills with seeds for the birds.
They make a sort of dance
as they descend and light
and fly off at a slant
across the strictly divided
black sash. At first
they came fearfully, worried
by the man's movements
inside the room. They watched
his eyes, and flew
when he looked. Now they expect
no harm from him
and forget he's there.
They come into his vision,
unafraid. He keeps
a certain distance and quietness
in tribute to them.
That they ignore him
he takes in tribute to himself.
But they stay cautious
of each other, half afraid, unwilling
to be too close. They snatch

what they can carry and fly
into the trees. They flirt out
with tail or beak and waste
more sometimes then they eat.
And the man, knowing
the price of seed, wishes
they would take more care.
But they understand only
what is free, and he
can give only as they
will take. Thus they have
enlightened him. He buys
the seed, to make it free.

8.

The river is rising,
approaching the window
in awful nearness.
Over it the air holds
a tense premonition
of the water's dark body
living where yesterday
things breathed. As he works
through the morning
the man has trouble
in the corner of his eye,
whole trees turning
in the channel as they go by,
the currents loaded
with the trash of the woods
and the trash of towns,
bearing down, and rising.

9.

There is a sort of vertical
geography that portions his life.

Outside, the chickadees
and titmice scrounge
his sunflower seed. The cardinals
feed like fires on mats of drift
lying on the currents
of the swollen river.
The air is a bridge
and they are free. He imagines
a necessary joy
in things that must fly
to eat. He is set apart
by the black grid of the window
and, below it, the table
of the contents of his mind:
notes and remnants,
uncompleted work,
unanswered mail,
unread books
—the subjects of conscience,
his yoke-fellow,
whose whispered accounting
has stopped one ear, leaving him
half deaf to the world.
Some pads of paper,
eleven pencils,
a leaky pen,
a jar of ink
are his powers. He'll
never fly.

10.

Rising, the river
is wild. There is no end
to what one may imagine
whose lands and buildings
lie in its reach. To one

who has felt his little boat
taken this way and that
in the braided currents
it is beyond speech.
"What's the river doing?"
"Coming up."
In Port Royal, that begins
a submergence of minds.
Heads are darkened.
To the man at work
through the mornings
in the long-legged cabin
above the water, there is
an influence of the rise
that he feels in his footsoles
and in his belly
even when he thinks
of something else. The window
looks out, like a word,
upon the wordless, fact
dissolving into mystery, darkness
overtaking light.
And the water reaches a height
it can only fall from, leaving
the tree trunks wet.
It has made a roof
to its rising, and become
a domestic thing.
It lies down in its place
like a horse in his stall.
Facts emerge from it:
drift it has hung in the trees,
stranded cans and bottles,
new carving in the banks
—a place of change, changed.
It leaves a mystic plane

in the air, a membrane
of history stretched between
the silt-lines on the banks,
a depth that for months
the man will go from his window
down into, knowing
he goes within the reach
of a dark power: where
the birds are, fish
were.

11.

How fine
to have a long-legged house
with a many-glassed window
looking out on the river
—and the wren singing
on a winter morning! How fine
to sweep the floor,
opening the doors
to let the air change,
and then to sit down
in the freshened room,
day pouring in the window!
But this is only for a while.
This house was not always
here. Another stood
in its place, and weathered
and grew old. He tore it down
and used the good of it
to build this. And farther on
another stood
that is gone. Nobody
alive now knows
how it looked, though some
recall a springhouse

that is gone too now. The stones
strew the pasture grass
where a roan colt grazes
and lifts his head to snort
at commotions in the wind.
All passes, and the man
at work in the house
has mostly ceased to mind.
There will be pangs
of ending, and he regrets
the terrors men bring to men.
But all passes—there is even
a kind of solace in that.
He has imagined animals
grazing at nightfall
on the place where his house stands.
Already his spirit
is with them, with a strange attentiveness,
hearing the grass
quietly tearing as they graze.

12.

The country where he lives
is haunted
by the ghost of an old forest.
In the cleared fields
where he gardens
and pastures his horses
it stood once,
and will return. There will be
a resurrection of the wild.
Already it stands in wait
at the pasture fences.
It is rising up
in the waste places of the cities.
When the fools of the capitals

have devoured each other
in righteousness,
and the machines have eaten
the rest of us, then
there will be the second coming
of the trees. They will come
straggling over the fences
slowly, but soon enough.
The highways will sound
with the feet of the wild herds,
returning. Beaver will ascend
the streams as the trees
close over them.
The wolf and the panther
will find their old ways
through the nights. Water
and air will flow clear.
Certain calamities
will have passed,
and certain pleasures.
The wind will do without
corners. How difficult
to think of it: miles and miles
and no window.

13.
Sometimes he thinks the earth
might be better without humans.
He's ashamed of that.
It worries him,
him being a human, and needing
to think well of the others
in order to think well of himself.
And there are
a few he thinks well of,
a few he loves

as well as himself almost,
and he would like to say
better. But history
is so largely unforgivable.
And now his mighty government
wants to help everybody
even if it has to kill them
to do it—like the fellow in the story
who helped his neighbor to Heaven:
"I heard the Lord calling him,
Judge, and I sent him on."
According to the government
everybody is just waiting
to be given a chance
to be like us. He can't
go along with that.
Here is a thing, flesh of his flesh,
that he hates. He would like
a little assurance
that no one will destroy the world
for some good cause.
Until he dies, he would like his life
to pertain to the earth.
But there is something in him
that will wait, even
while he protests,
for things turn out as they will.
Out his window this morning
he saw nine ducks in flight,
and a hawk dive at his mate
in delight.
The day stands apart
from the calendar. There is a will
that receives it as enough.
He is given a fragment of time
in this fragment of the world.
He likes it pretty well.

14.

The longest night is past.
It is the blessed morning of the year.
Beyond the window, snow
in patches on the river bank,
frosty sunlight on the dry corn,
and buds on the water maples
red, red in the cold.

15.

The sycamore gathers
out of the sky, white
in the glance that looks up to it
through the black crisscross
of the window. But it is not a glance
that it offers itself to.
It is no lightning stroke
caught in the eye. It stays,
an old holding in place.
And its white is not so pure
as a glance would have it,
but emerges partially,
the tree's renewal of itself,
among the mottled browns
and olives of the old bark.
Its dazzling comes into the sun
a little at a time
as though a god in it
is slowly revealing himself.
How often the man of the window
has studied its motley trunk,
the out-starting of its branches,
its smooth crotches,
its revelations of whiteness,
hoping to see beyond his glances,
the distorting geometry
of preconception and habit,

to know it beyond words.
All he has learned of it
does not add up to it.
There is a bird who nests in it
in the summer and seems to sing of it—
the quick lights among its leaves
—better than he can.
It is not by his imagining
its whiteness comes.
The world is greater than its words.
To speak of it the mind must bend.

16.

His mind gone from the window
into dark thought, suddenly
a flash of water
lights in the corner of his eye:
the kingfisher is rising,
laden, out of his plunge,
the water still subsiding
under the bare willow.
The window becomes a part
of his mind's history, the entrance
of days into it. And awake
now, watching the water flow
beyond the glass, his mind
is watched by a spectre of itself
that is a window on the past.
Life steadily adding
its subtractions, it has fallen
to him to remember
an old man who, dying,
dreamed of his garden,
a harvest so bountiful
he couldn't carry it home
—another who saw

in the flaws of the moon
a woman's face
like a cameo.

17.

For a night and a day
his friend stayed here
on his way across the continent.
In the afternoon they walked
down from Port Royal
to the river, following
for a while the fall of Camp Branch
through the woods,
then crossing the ridge
and entering the woods again
on the valley rim. They talked
of history—men who saw visions
of crops where the woods stood
and stand again, the crops
gone. They ate the cold apples
they carried in their pockets.
They lay on a log in the sun
to rest, looking up
through bare branches at the sky.
They saw a nuthatch walk
in a loop on the side of a tree
in a late patch of light
while below them the *Lexington*
shoved sand up the river,
her diesels shaking the air.
They walked along trees
across ravines. Now his friend
is back on the highway, and he sits again
at his window. Another day.
During the night snow fell.

18.

The window grows fragile
in a time of war.
The man seated beneath it
feels its glass turn deadly.
He feels the nakedness
of his face and throat.
Its shards and splinters balance
in transparence, delicately
seamed. In the violence
of men against men, it will not last.
In any mind turned away
in hate, it will go blind,
Men spare one another
by will. When there is hate
it is joyous to kill. And he
has borne the hunger to destroy,
riding anger like a captain,
savage, exalted and blind.
There is war in his veins
like a loud song.
He has known his heart to rise
in glad holocaust against his kind,
and felt hard in thigh and arm
the thew of fury.

19.

Peace. May he waken
not too late from his wraths
to find his window still
clear in its wall, and the world
there. Within things
there is peace, and at the end
of things. It is the mind
turned away from the world
that turns against it.

The armed presidents stand
on deadly islands in the air,
overshadowing the crops.
Peace. Let men, who cannot be brothers
to themselves, be brothers
to mulleins and daisies
that have learned to live on the earth.
Let them understand the pride
of sycamores and thrushes
that receive the light gladly, and do not
think to illuminate themselves.
Let them know that the foxes and the owls
are joyous in their lives,
and their gayety is praise to the heavens,
and they do not raven with their minds.
In the night the devourer,
and in the morning all things
find the light a comfort.
Peace. The earth turns
against all living, in the end.
And when mind has not outraged
itself against its nature,
they die and become the place
they lived in. Peace to the bones
that walk in the sun toward death,
for they will come to it soon enough.
Let the phoebes return in spring
and build their nest of moss
in the porch rafters,
and in autumn let them depart.
Let the garden be planted,
and let the frost come.
Peace to the porch and the garden.
Peace to the man in the window.

20

In the early morning dark
he dreamed of the spring woodsflowers
standing in the ground,
dark yet under the leaves and under
the bare cold branches.
But in his dream he knew their way
was prepared, and in their time
they would rise up joyful.
And though he had dreamed earlier
of strife, his sleep became peaceful.
He said: If we, who have killed
our brothers and hated ourselves,
are made in the image of God,
then surely the bloodroot,
wild phlox, trillium and mayapple
are more truly made
in God's image, for they have desired
to be no more than they are,
and they have spared each other.
Their future
is undiminished by their past.
Let me, he said in his dream,
become always less a soldier
and more a man,
for what is unopened in the ground
is pledged to peace.
When he woke and went out
a flock of wild ducks that had fed
on the river while he slept
flew off in fear of him.
And he walked, manly, into the new day.
He came to his window
where he sat and looked out,
the earth before him, blessed
by his dream of peace,
bad history behind him.

21.

He has known a tunnel
through the falling snow
that brought him back at dark
and nearly killed him on the way,
the road white as the sky
and the snow piling.
Mortality crept up close
in the darkness round his eyes.
He felt his death's wrenched avatars
lying like silent animals
along the ditch. He thought
of his wife, his supper and his bed,
and kept on, and made it.
Now he sits at the window
again, the country hard and bright
in this winter's coldest morning.
The river, unfrozen still,
gives off a breath of smoke
that flows upstream with the wind.
Behind him that burrow
along the wild road
grows certain in his mind,
leading here, surely. It has arrived
at the window, and is clarified.
Now he has learned another way
he can come here. Luck
taught him, and desire.
The snow lies under the woods
and February is ending.
Far off, another way, he hears
the flute of spring,
an old-style traveler,
wandering through the trees.

22.

Still sleeping, he heard
the phoebe call, and woke to it,
and winter passed out of his mind.
The bird, in the high branches
above the road-culvert mouth,
sang to what was sleeping,
two notes, clear and
harsh. The stream came,
full-voiced, down the rocks
out of the woods. The wood ducks
have come back to nest
in the old hollow sycamore.
The window has changed, no longer
remembering, but waiting.

23.

He stood on the ground
and saw his wife borne away
in the air, and suddenly
knew her. It is not the sky
he trusts her to, or her flight,
but to herself as he saw her
turn back and smile. And he
turned back to the buried garden
where the spring flood rose.
The window is made strange
by these days he has come to.
She is the comfort of the rooms
she leaves behind her.

24.

His love returns
and walks among the trees,
a new time lying beneath
the leaves at her feet.
There are songs in the ground

audible to her. She enters
the dark globe of sleep,
waking the tree frogs
whose songs star the silence
in constellations. She wakens
the birds of mornings. The sun
makes a low gentle piping.
The bloodroot rises in its folded
leaf, and there is a tensing
in the woods. There is
no window where she is.
All is clear where the light begins
to dress the branch in green.

25.

The bloodroot is white
in the woods, and men renew
their abuse of the world
and each other. Abroad
we burn and maim
in the name of principles
we no longer recognize in acts.
At home our flayed land
flows endlessly
to burial in the sea.
When mortality is not heavy
on us, humanity is—
public meaninglessness
preying on private meaning.
As the weather warms, the driven
swarm into the river,
pursued by whining engines,
missing the world
as they pass over it,
every man
his own mosquito.

26.

In the heron's eye
is one of the dies of change.
Another
is in the sun.
Each thing is carried
beyond itself.
The man of the window
lives at the edge,
knowing the approach
of what must be, joy
and dread.
Now the old sycamore
yields at its crown
a dead branch.
It will sink like evening
into its standing place.
The young trees rise,
and the dew is on them,
and the heat of the day
is on them, and the dark
— end and beginning
without end.

27.

Now that April with sweet rain
has come to Port William again,
Burley Coulter rows out
on the river to fish.
He sits all day in his boat,
tied to a willow, his hat
among green branches,
his dark line curving
in the wind. He is one
with the sun.
The current's horses graze

in the shade along the banks.
The watcher leaves his window
and goes out.
He sits in the woods, watched
by more than he sees.
What is his is
past. He has come
to a roofless place
and a windowless.
There is a wild light
his mind loses
until the spring renews,
but it holds his mind
and will not let it rest.
The window is a fragment
of the world suspended
in the world, the known
adrift in mystery.
And now the green
rises. The window has an edge
that is celestial,
where the eyes are surpassed.

TO A SIBERIAN WOODSMAN
(after looking at some pictures in a magazine)

You lean at ease in your warm house at night after supper,
listening to your daughter play the accordion. You smile
with the pleasure of a man confident in his hands, resting
after a day of long labor in the forest, the cry of the saw
in your head, and the vision of coming home to rest.
Your daughter's face is clear in the joy of hearing
her own music. Her fingers live on the keys
like people familiar with the land they were born in.

You sit at the dinner table late into the night with your son,
tying the bright flies that will lead you along the forest streams.
Over you, as your hands work, is the dream of the still pools.
        Over you is the dream
of your silence while the east brightens, birds waking close by
        you in the trees.

2.

I have thought of you stepping out of your doorway at dawn,
        your son in your tracks.
You go in under the overarching green branches of the forest
whose ways, strange to me, are well known to you as the sound
        of your own voice
or the silence that lies around you now that you have ceased to
        speak,
and soon the voice of the stream rises ahead of you, and you
        take the path beside it.
I have thought of the sun breaking pale through the mists over
        you
as you come to the pool where you will fish, and of the mist
        drifting
over the water, and of the cast fly resting light on the face of the
        pool.

3.

And I am here in Kentucky in the place I have made myself
in the world. I sit on my porch above the river that flows muddy
and slow along the feet of the trees. I hear the voices of the wren
and the yellow-throated warbler whose songs pass near the
            windows
and over the roof. In my house my daughter learns the
            womanhood
of her mother. My son is at play, pretending to be
the man he believes I am. I am the outbreathing of this ground.
My words are its words as the wren's song is its song.

4.

Who has invented our enmity? Who has prescribed us
hatred of each other? Who has armed us against each other
with the death of the world? Who has appointed me such anger
that I should desire the burning of your house or the
            destruction of your children?
Who has appointed such anger to you? Who has set loose the
            thought
that we should oppose each other with the ruin of forests and
            rivers, and the silence of birds?
Who has said to us that the voices of my land shall be strange
to you, and the voices of your land strange to me?

Who has imagined that I would destroy myself in order to
            destroy you,
or that I could improve myself by destroying you? Who has
            imagined
that your death could be negligible to me now that I have seen
            these pictures of your face?
Who has imagined that I would not speak familiarly with you,
or laugh with you, or visit in your house and go to work with
            you in the forest?
And now one of the ideas of my place will be that you would
            gladly talk and visit and work with me.

5.

I sit in the shade of the trees of the land I was born in.
As they are native I am native, and I hold to this place as
       carefully as they hold to it.
I do not see the national flag flying from the staff of the
       sycamore,
or any decree of the government written on the leaves of the
       walnut,
nor has the elm bowed before the monuments or sworn the oath
       of allegiance.
They have not declared to whom they stand in welcome.

6.

In the thought of you I imagine myself free of the weapons and
       the official hates that I have borne on my back like a
       hump,
and in the thought of myself I imagine you free of weapons and
       official hates,
so that if we should meet we would not go by each other
       looking at the ground like slaves sullen under their
       burdens,
but would stand clear in the gaze of each other.

7.

There is no government so worthy as your son who fishes with
       you in silence beside the forest pool.
There is no national glory so comely as your daughter whose
       hands have learned a music and go their own way on the
       keys.
There is no national glory so comely as my daughter who
       dances and sings and is the brightness of
       my house.
There is no government so worthy as my son who laughs, as he
       comes up the path from the river in the evening, for joy.

A DISCIPLINE

Turn toward the holocaust, it approaches
on every side, there is no other place
to turn. Dawning in your veins
is the light of the blast
that will print your shadow on stone
in a last antic of despair
to survive you in the dark.
Man has put his history to sleep
in the engine of doom. It flies
over his dreams in the night,
a blazing cocoon. O gaze into the fire
and be consumed with man's despair,
and be still, and wait. And then see
the world go on with the patient work
of seasons, embroidering birdsong
upon itself as for a wedding, and feel
your heart set out in the morning
like a young traveler, arguing the world
from the kiss of a pretty girl.
It is the time's discipline to think
of the death of all living, and yet live.

A POEM OF THANKS

I have been spared another day
to come into this night
as though there is a mercy in things
mindful of me. Love, cast all
thought aside. I cast aside
all thought. Our bodies enter
their brief precedence,
surrounded by their sleep.
Through you I rise, and you
through me, into the joy
we make, but may not keep.

❁❁❁❁❁❁❁❁❁

ENVOY

Love, all day there has been at the edge of my mind
the wish that my life would hurry on,
my days pass quickly and be done,
for I felt myself a man carrying a loose tottering bundle
along a narrow scaffold: if I could carry it
fast enough, I could hold it together to the end.

Now, leaving my perplexity and haste,
I come within the boundaries of your life, an interior
clear and calm. You could not admit me burdened.
I approach you clean as a child of all that has been with me.
You speak to me in the dark tongue of my joy
that you do not know. In you I know
the deep leisure of the filling moon. May I live long.

FARMING: A HAND BOOK

(1970)

For Owen and Loyce Flood

THE MAN BORN TO FARMING

The grower of trees, the gardener, the man born to farming,
whose hands reach into the ground and sprout,
to him the soil is a divine drug. He enters into death
yearly, and comes back rejoicing. He has seen the light lie down
in the dung heap, and rise again in the corn.
His thought passes along the row ends like a mole.
What miraculous seed has he swallowed
that the unending sentence of his love flows out of his mouth
like a vine clinging in the sunlight, and like water
descending in the dark?

THE STONES

I owned a slope full of stones.
Like buried pianos they lay in the ground,
shards of old sea-ledges, stumbling blocks
where the earth caught and kept them
dark, an old music mute in them
that my head keeps now I have dug them out.
I broke them where they slugged in their dark
cells, and lifted them up in pieces.
As I piled them in the light
I began their music. I heard their old lime
rouse in breath of song that has not left me.
I gave pain and weariness to their bearing out.
What bond have I made with the earth,
having worn myself against it? It is a fatal singing
I have carried with me out of that day.
The stones have given me music
that figures for me their holes in the earth
and their long lying in them dark.
They have taught me the weariness that loves the ground,
and I must prepare a fitting silence.

THE SUPPLANTING

Where the road came, no longer bearing men,
but briars, honeysuckle, buckbush and wild grape,
the house fell to ruin, and only the old wife's daffodils
rose in spring among the wild vines to be domestic
and to keep the faith, and her peonies drenched the tangle
with white bloom. For a while in the years of its wilderness
a wayfaring drunk slept clinched to the floor there
in the cold nights. And then I came, and set fire
to the remnants of house and shed, and let time
hurry in the flame. I fired it so that all
would burn, and watched the blaze settle on the waste
like a shawl. I knew those old ones departed
then, and I arrived. As the fire fed, I felt rise in me
something that would not bear my name — something that
                    bears us
through the flame, and is lightened of us, and is glad.

❀❀❀❀❀❀❀❀❀

SOWING

In the stilled place that once was a road going down
from the town to the river, and where the lives of marriages grew
a house, cistern and barn, flowers, the tilted stone of borders,
and the deeds of their lives ran to neglect, and honeysuckle
and then the fire overgrew it all, I walk heavy
with seed, spreading on the cleared hill the beginnings
of green, clover and grass to be pasture. Between
history's death upon the place and the trees that would
                    have come
I claim, and act, and am mingled in the fate of the world.

THE FAMILIAR

The hand is risen from the earth,
the sap risen, leaf come back to branch,
bird to nest crotch. Beans lift
their heads up in the row. The known
returns to be known again. Going
and coming back, it forms its curves,
a nerved ghostly anatomy in the air.

❦❦❦❦❦❦

THE FARMER AMONG THE TOMBS

I am oppressed by all the room taken up by the dead,
their headstones standing shoulder to shoulder,
the bones imprisoned under them.
Plow up the graveyards! Haul off the monuments!
Pry open the vaults and the coffins
so the dead may nourish their graves
and go free, their acres traversed all summer
by crop rows and cattle and foraging bees.

FOR THE REBUILDING OF A HOUSE

To know the inhabiting reasons
of trees and streams, old men
who shed their lives
on the world like leaves,
I watch them go.
And I go. I build
the place of my leaving.

The days arc into vision
like fish leaping, their shining
caught in the stream.
I watch them go
in homage and sorrow.
I build the place of my dream.
I build the place of my leaving
that the dark may come clean.

❧❧❧❧❧❧

THE SPRINGS

In a country without saints or shrines
I know one who made his pilgrimage
to springs, where in his life's dry years
his mind held on. Everlasting,
people called them, and gave them names.
The water broke into sounds and shinings
at the vein mouth, bearing the taste
of the place, the deep rock, sweetness
out of the dark. He knelt and drank
in bondage to the ground.

RAIN

It is a day of the earth's renewing without any man's doing or
         help.
Though I have fields I do not go out to work in them.
Though I have crops standing in rows I do not go out
to look at them or gather what has ripened or hoe the weeds
         from the balks.
Though I have animals I stay dry in the house while they graze
         in the wet.
Though I have buildings they stand closed under their roofs.
Though I have fences they go without me.
My life stands in place, covered, like a hayrick or a mushroom.

✿❯✿❯✿❯✿❯✿

SLEEP

I love to lie down weary
under the stalk of sleep
growing slowly out of my head,
the dark leaves meshing.

TO KNOW THE DARK

To go in the dark with a light is to know the light.
To know the dark, go dark. Go without sight,
and find that the dark, too, blooms and sings,
and is traveled by dark feet and dark wings.

❀❁❀❁❀❁❀❁❀❁

WINTER NIGHT POEM FOR MARY

As I started home after dark
I looked into the sky and saw the new moon,
an old man with a basket on his arm.
He walked among the cedars in the bare woods.
They stood like guardians, dark
as he passed. He might have been singing,
or he might not. He might have been sowing
the spring flowers, or he might not. But I saw him
with his basket, going along the hilltop.

WINTER NIGHTFALL

The fowls speak and sing, settling for the night.
The mare shifts in the bedding.
In her womb her foal sleeps and grows,
within and within and within. Her jaw grinds,
meditative in the fragrance of timothy.
Soon now my own rest will come.
The silent river flows on in the dusk, miles and miles.
Outside the walls and on the roof and in the woods
the cold rain falls.

❁❁❁❁❁❁❁❁

FEBRUARY 2, 1968

In the dark of the moon, in flying snow, in the dead of winter,
war spreading, families dying, the world in danger,
I walk the rocky hillside, sowing clover.

MARCH 22, 1968

As spring begins the river rises,
filling like the sorrow of nations
—uprooted trees, soil of squandered mountains,
the debris of kitchens, all passing
seaward. At dawn snow began to fall.
The ducks, moving north, pass
like shadows through the falling white.
The jonquils, half open, bend down with its weight.
The plow freezes in the furrow.
In the night I lay awake, thinking
of the river rising, the spring heavy
with official meaningless deaths.

THE MORNING'S NEWS

To moralize the state, they drag out a man,
and bind his hands, and darken his eyes
with a black rag to be free of the light in them,
and tie him to a post, and kill him.
And I am sickened by complicity in my race.
To kill in hot savagery like a beast
is understandable. It is forgivable and curable.
But to kill by design, deliberately, without wrath,
that is the sullen labor that perfects Hell.
The serpent is gentle, compared to man.
It is man, the inventor of cold violence,
death as waste, who has made himself lonely
among the creatures, and set himself aside,
so that he cannot work in the sun with hope,
or sit at peace in the shade of any tree.
The morning's news drives sleep out of the head
at night. Uselessness and horror hold the eyes
open to the dark. Weary, we lie awake
in the agony of the old giving birth to the new
without assurance that the new will be better.
I look at my son, whose eyes are like a young god's,
they are so open to the world.
I look at my sloping fields now turning
green with the young grass of April. What must I do
to go free? I think I must put on
a deathlier knowledge, and prepare to die
rather than enter into the design of man's hate.
I will purge my mind of the airy claims
of church and state. I will serve the earth
and not pretend my life could better serve.
Another morning comes with its strange cure.
The earth is news. Though the river floods
and the spring is cold, my heart goes on,
faithful to a mystery in a cloud,
and the summer's garden continues its descent
through me, toward the ground.

ENRICHING THE EARTH

To enrich the earth I have sowed clover and grass
to grow and die. I have plowed in the seeds
of winter grains and of various legumes,
their growth to be plowed in to enrich the earth.
I have stirred into the ground the offal
and the decay of the growth of past seasons
and so mended the earth and made its yield increase.
All this serves the dark. I am slowly falling
into the fund of things. And yet to serve the earth,
not knowing what I serve, gives a wideness
and a delight to the air, and my days
do not wholly pass. It is the mind's service,
for when the will fails so do the hands
and one lives at the expense of life.
After death, willing or not, the body serves,
entering the earth. And so what was heaviest
and most mute is at last raised up into song.

A WET TIME

The land is an ark, full of things waiting.
Underfoot it goes temporary and soft, tracks
filling with water as the foot is raised.
The fields, sodden, go free of plans. Hands
become obscure in their use, prehistoric.
The mind passes over changed surfaces
like a boat, drawn to the thought of roofs
and to the thought of swimming and wading birds.
Along the river croplands and gardens
are buried in the flood, airy places grown dark
and silent beneath it. Under the slender branch
holding the new nest of the hummingbird
the river flows heavy with earth, the water
turned the color of broken slopes. I stand
deep in the mud of the shore, a stake
planted to measure the rise, the water rising,
the earth falling to meet it. A great cottonwood
passes down, the leaves shivering as the roots
drag the bottom. I was not ready for this
parting, my native land putting out to sea.

THE SILENCE

What must a man do to be at home in the world?
There must be times when he is here
as though absent, gone beyond words into the woven shadows
of the grass and the flighty darknesses
of leaves shaking in the wind, and beyond
the sense of the weariness of engines and of his own heart,
his wrongs grown old unforgiven. It must be with him
as though his bones fade beyond thought
into the shadows that grow out of the ground
so that the furrow he opens in the earth opens
in his bones, and he hears the silence
of the tongues of the dead tribesmen buried here
a thousand years ago. And then what presences will rise up
before him, weeds bearing flowers, and the dry wind
rain! What songs he will hear!

IN THIS WORLD

The hill pasture, an open place among the trees,
tilts into the valley. The clovers and tall grasses
are in bloom. Along the foot of the hill
dark floodwater moves down the river.
The sun sets. Ahead of nightfall the birds sing.
I have climbed up to water the horses
and now sit and rest, high on the hillside,
letting the day gather and pass. Below me
cattle graze out across the wide fields of the bottomlands,
slow and preoccupied as stars. In this world
men are making plans, wearing themselves out,
spending their lives, in order to kill each other.

※-(-※-(-※-(-※-(-※-(-※

THE NEW ROOF

On the housetop, the floor of the boundless
where birds and storms fly and disappear,
and the valley opened over our heads, a leap
of clarity between the hills, we bent five days
in the sun, tearing free the old roof, nailing on
the new, letting the sun touch for once
in fifty years the dusky rafters, and then
securing the house again in its shelter and shade.
Thus like a little ledge a piece of my history
has come between me and the sky.

A PRAISE

His memories lived in the place
like fingers locked in the rock ledges
like roots. When he died
and his influence entered the air
I said, Let my mind be the earth
of his thought, let his kindness
go ahead of me. Though I do not escape
the history barbed in my flesh,
certain wise movements of his hands,
the turns of his speech
keep with me. His hope of peace
keeps with me in harsh days,
the shell of his breath dimming away
three summers in the earth.

❧❧❧❧❧❧

ON THE HILL LATE AT NIGHT

The ripe grassheads bend in the starlight
in the soft wind, beneath them the darkness
of the grass, fathomless, the long blades
rising out of the well of time. Cars
travel the valley roads below me, their lights
finding the dark, and racing on. Above
their roar is a silence I have suddenly heard,
and felt the country turn under the stars
toward dawn. I am wholly willing to be here
between the bright silent thousands of stars
and the life of the grass pouring out of the ground.
The hill has grown to me like a foot.
Until I lift the earth I cannot move.

THE SEEDS

The seeds begin abstract as their species,
remote as the name on the sack
they are carried home in: Fayette Seed Company
Corner of Vine and Rose. But the sower
going forth to sow sets foot
into time to come, the seeds falling
on his own place. He has prepared a way
for his life to come to him, if it will.
Like a tree, he has given roots
to the earth, and stands free.

❁❁❁❁❁❁❁

THE WISH TO BE GENEROUS

All that I serve will die, all my delights,
the flesh kindled from my flesh, garden and field,
the silent lilies standing in the woods,
the woods, the hill, the whole earth, all
will burn in man's evil, or dwindle
in its own age. Let the world bring on me
the sleep of darkness without stars, so I may know
my little light taken from me into the seed
of the beginning and the end, so I may bow
to mystery, and take my stand on the earth
like a tree in a field, passing without haste
or regret toward what will be, my life
a patient willing descent into the grass.

AIR AND FIRE

From my wife and household and fields
that I have so carefully come to in my time
I enter the craziness of travel,
the reckless elements of air and fire.
Having risen up from my native land,
I find myself smiled at by beautiful women,
making me long for a whole life
to devote to each one, making love to her
in some house, in some way of sleeping
and waking I would make only for her.
And all over the country I find myself
falling in love with houses, woods, and farms
that I will never set foot in.
My eyes go wandering through America,
two wayfaring brothers, resting in silence
against the forbidden gates. O what if
an angel came to me, and said,
"Go free of what you have done. Take
what you want." The atoms of blood
and brain and bone strain apart
at the thought. What I am is the way home.
Like rest after a sleepless night,
my old love comes on me in midair.

THE LILIES

Amid the gray trunks of ancient trees we found
the gay woodland lilies nodding on their stems,
frail and fair, so delicately balanced the air
held or moved them as it stood or moved.
The ground that slept beneath us woke in them
and made a music of the light, as it had waked
and sung in fragile things unnumbered years,
and left their kind no less symmetrical and fair
for all that time. Does my land have the health
of this, where nothing falls but into life?

❈❈❈❈❈❈❈❈❈

INDEPENDENCE DAY

for Gene Meatyard

Between painting a roof yesterday and the hay
harvest tomorrow, a holiday in the woods
under the grooved trunks and branches, the roof
of leaves lighted and shadowed by the sky.
As America from England, the woods stands free
from politics and anthems. So in the woods I stand
free, knowing my land. My country, 'tis of the
drying pools along Camp Branch I sing
where the water striders walk like Christ,
all sons of God, and of the woods grown old
on the stony hill where the thrush's song rises
in the light like a curling vine and the bobwhite's
whistle opens in the air, broad and pointed as a leaf.

A STANDING GROUND

Flee fro the prees, and dwelle with sothfastnesse;
Suffyce unto thy thyng, though hit be smal . . .

However just and anxious I have been,
I will stop and step back
from the crowd of those who may agree
with what I say, and be apart.
There is no earthly promise of life or peace
but where the roots branch and weave
their patient silent passages in the dark;
uprooted, I have been furious without an aim.
I am not bound for any public place,
but for ground of my own
where I have planted vines and orchard trees,
and in the heat of the day climbed up
into the healing shadow of the woods.
Better than any argument is to rise at dawn
and pick dew-wet red berries in a cup.

SONG IN A YEAR OF CATASTROPHE

I began to be followed by a voice saying:
"It can't last. It can't last.
Harden yourself. Harden yourself.
Be ready. Be ready."

"Go look under the leaves,"
it said, "for what is living there
is long dead in your tongue."
And it said, "Put your hands
into the earth. Live close
to the ground. Learn the darkness.
Gather round you all
the things that you love, name
their names, prepare
to lose them. It will be
as if all you know were turned
around within your body."

And I went and put my hands
into the ground, and they took root
and grew into a season's harvest.
I looked behind the veil
of the leaves, and heard voices
that I knew had been dead
in my tongue years before my birth.
I learned the dark.

And still the voice stayed with me.
Waking in the early mornings,
I could hear it, like a bird
bemused among the leaves,
a mockingbird idly singing
in the autumn of catastrophe:
"Be ready. Be ready.
Harden yourself. Harden yourself."

And I heard the sound
of a great engine pounding
in the air, and a voice asking:
"Change or slavery?
Hardship or slavery?"
and voices answering:
"Slavery! Slavery!"
And I was afraid, loving
what I knew would be lost.

Then the voice following me said:
"You have not yet come close enough.
Come nearer the ground. Learn
from the woodcock in the woods
whose feathering is a ritual
of the fallen leaves,
and from the nesting quail
whose speckling makes her hard to see
in the long grass.
Study the coat of the mole.
For the farmer shall wear
the furrows and the greenery
of his fields, and bear
the long standing of the woods."

And I asked: "You mean death, then?"
"Yes," the voice said. "Die
into what the earth requires of you."
I let go all holds then, and sank
like a hopeless swimmer into the earth,
and at last came fully into the ease
and the joy of that place,
all my lost ones returning.

9/28/68

THE CURRENT

Having once put his hand into the ground,
seeding there what he hopes will outlast him,
a man has made a marriage with his place,
and if he leaves it his flesh will ache to go back.
His hand has given up its birdlife in the air.
It has reached into the dark like a root
and begun to wake, quick and mortal, in timelessness,
a flickering sap coursing upward into his head
so that he sees the old tribespeople bend
in the sun, digging with sticks, the forest opening
to receive their hills of corn, squash, and beans,
their lodges and graves, and closing again.
He is made their descendant, what they left
in the earth rising into him like a seasonal juice.
And he sees the bearers of his own blood arriving,
the forest burrowing into the earth as they come,
their hands gathering the stones up into walls,
and relaxing, the stones crawling back into the ground
to lie still under the black wheels of machines.
The current flowing to him through the earth
flows past him, and he sees one descended from him,
a young man who has reached into the ground,
his hand held in the dark as by a hand.

THE MAD FARMER REVOLUTION

*being a fragment
of the natural history of New Eden,
in homage
to Mr. Ed McClanahan, one of the locals*

The mad farmer, the thirsty one,
went dry. When he had time
he threw a visionary high
lonesome on the holy communion wine.
"It is an awesome event
when an earthen man has drunk
his fill of the blood of a god,"
people said, and got out of his way.
He plowed the churchyard, the
minister's wife, three graveyards
and a golf course. In a parking lot
he planted a forest of little pines.
He sanctified the groves,
dancing at night in the oak shades
with goddesses. He led
a field of corn to creep up
and tassel like an Indian tribe
on the courthouse lawn. Pumpkins
ran out to the ends of their vines
to follow him. Ripe plums
and peaches reached into his pockets.
Flowers sprang up in his tracks
everywhere he stepped. And then
his planter's eye fell on
that parson's fair fine lady
again. "O holy plowman," cried she,
"I am all grown up in weeds.
Pray, bring me back into good tilth."
He tilled her carefully

and laid her by, and she
did bring forth others of her kind,
and others, and some more.
They sowed and reaped till all
the countryside was filled
with farmers and their brides sowing
and reaping. When they died
they became two spirits of the woods.

THE CONTRARINESS OF THE MAD FARMER

I am done with apologies. If contrariness is my
inheritance and destiny, so be it. If it is my mission
to go in at exits and come out at entrances, so be it.
I have planted by the stars in defiance of the experts,
and tilled somewhat by incantation and by singing,
and reaped, as I knew, by luck and Heaven's favor,
in spite of the best advice. If I have been caught
so often laughing at funerals, that was because
I knew the dead were already slipping away,
preparing a comeback, and can I help it?
And if at weddings I have gritted and gnashed
my teeth, it was because I knew where the bridegroom
had sunk his manhood, and knew it would not
be resurrected by a piece of cake. "Dance," they told me,
and I stood still, and while they stood
quiet in line at the gate of the Kingdom, I danced.
"Pray," they said, and I laughed, covering myself
in the earth's brightnesses, and then stole off gray
into the midst of a revel, and prayed like an orphan.
When they said, "I know that my Redeemer liveth,"
I told them, "He's dead." And when they told me,
"God is dead," I answered, "He goes fishing every day
in the Kentucky River. I see Him often."
When they asked me would I like to contribute
I said no, and when they had collected
more than they needed, I gave them as much as I had.
When they asked me to join them I wouldn't,
and then went off by myself and did more
than they would have asked. "Well, then," they said,
"go and organize the International Brotherhood
of Contraries," and I said, "Did you finish killing
everybody who was against peace?" So be it.
Going against men, I have heard at times a deep harmony
thrumming in the mixture, and when they ask me what,
I say I don't know. It is not the only or the easiest
way to come to the truth. It is one way.

THE FARMER AND THE SEA

The sea always arriving,
hissing in pebbles, is breaking
its edge where the landsman
squats on his rock. The dark
of the earth is familiar to him,
close mystery of his source
and end, always flowering
in the light and always
fading. But the dark of the sea
is perfect and strange,
the absence of any place,
immensity on the loose.
Still, he sees it is another
keeper of the land, caretaker,
shaking the earth, breaking it,
clicking the pieces, but somewhere
holding deep fields yet to rise,
shedding its richness on them
silently as snow, keeper and maker
of places wholly dark. And in him
something dark applauds.

EARTH AND FIRE

In this woman the earth speaks.
Her words open in me, cells of light
flashing in my body, and make a song
that I follow toward her out of my need.
The pain I have given her I wear
like another skin, tender, the air
around me flashing with thorns.
And yet such joy as I have given her
sings in me and is part of her song.
The winds of her knees shake me
like a flame. I have risen up from her,
time and again, a new man.

THE MAD FARMER IN THE CITY

". . . a field woman is a portion
of the field; she has somehow lost
her own margin . . ." THOMAS HARDY

As my first blow against it, I would not stay.
As my second, I learned to live without it.
As my third, I went back one day and saw
that my departure had left a little hole
where some of its strength was flowing out,
and I heard the earth singing beneath the street.
Singing quietly myself, I followed the song
among the traffic. Everywhere I went, singing,
following the song, the stones cracked,
and I heard it stronger. I heard it strongest
in the presence of women. There was one I met
who had the music of the ground in her, and she
was its dancer. "O Exile," I sang, "for want of you
there is a tree that has borne no leaves
and a planting season that will not turn warm."
Looking at her, I felt a tightening of roots
under the pavement, and I turned and went
with her a little way, dancing beside her.
And I saw a black woman still inhabiting
as in a dream the space of the open fields
where she had bent to plant and gather. She stood
rooted in the music I heard, pliant and proud
as a stalk of wheat with the grain heavy. No man
with the city thrusting angles in his brain
is equal to her. To reach her he must tear it down.
Wherever lovely women are the city is undone,
its geometry broken in pieces and lifted,
its streets and corners fading like mist at sunrise
above groves and meadows and planted fields.

THE BIRTH (NEAR PORT WILLIAM)

They were into the lambing, up late.
Talking and smoking around their lantern,
they squatted in the barn door, left open
so the quiet of the winter night
diminished what they said. The chill
had begun to sink into their clothes.
Now and then they raised their hands
to breathe on them. The youngest one
yawned and shivered.

      "Damn," he said,
"I'd like to be asleep. I'd like to be
curled up in a warm nest like an old
groundhog, and sleep till spring."

"When I was your age, Billy, it wasn't
sleep I thought about," Uncle Stanley said.
"Last few years here I've took to sleeping."

And Raymond said: "To sleep till spring
you'd have to have a trust in things
the way animals do. Been a long time,
I reckon, since people felt safe enough
to sleep more than a night. You might
wake up someplace you didn't go to sleep at."

They hushed a while, as if to let the dark
brood on what they had said. Behind them
a sheep stirred in the bedding and coughed.
It was getting close to midnight.
Later they would move back along the row
of penned ewes, making sure the newborn
lambs were well dried, and had sucked,

and then they would go home cold to bed.
The barn stood between the ridgetop
and the woods along the bluff. Below
was the valley floor and the river
they could not see. They could hear
the wind dragging its underside
through the bare branches of the woods.
And suddenly the wind began to carry
a low singing. They looked across
the lantern at each other's eyes
and saw they all had heard. They stood,
their huge shadows rising up around them.
The night had changed. They were already
on their way—dry leaves underfoot
and mud under the leaves—to another barn
on down along the woods' edge,
an old stripping room, where by the light
of the open stove door they saw the man,
and then the woman and the child
lying on a bed of straw on the dirt floor.

"Well, look a there," the old man said.
"First time this ever happened here."

And Billy, looking, and looking away,
said: "Howdy. Howdy. Bad night."

And Raymond said: "There's a first
time, they say, for everything."

                    And that
he thought, was as reassuring as anything
was likely to be, and as he needed it to be.
They did what they could. Not much.
They brought a piece of rug and some sacks
to ease the hard bed a little, and one

wedged three dollar bills into a crack
in the wall in a noticeable place.
And they stayed on, looking, looking away,
until finally the man said they were well
enough off, and should be left alone.
They went back to their sheep. For a while
longer they squatted by their lantern
and talked, tired, wanting sleep, yet stirred
by wonder—old Stanley too, though he would not
say so.

"Don't make no difference," he said.
"They'll have 'em anywhere. Looks like a man
would have a right to be born in bed, if not
die there, but he don't."

"But you heard
that singing in the wind," Billy said.
"What about that?"

"Ghosts. They do that way."

"Not that way."

"Scared him, it did."
The old man laughed. "We'll have to hold
his damn hand for him, and lead him home."

"It don't even bother you," Billy said.
"You go right on just the same. But you heard."

"Now that I'm old I sleep in the dark.
That ain't what I used to do in it. I heard
something."

"You heard a good deal more
than you'll understand," Raymond said,
"or him or me either."

They looked at him.
He had, they knew, a talent for unreasonable
belief. He could believe in tomorrow
before it became today—a human enough
failing, and they were tolerant.

He said:
"It's the old ground trying it again.
Solstice, seeding and birth—it never
gets enough. It wants the birth of a man
to bring together sky and earth, like a stalk
of corn. It's not death that makes the dead
rise out of the ground, but something alive
straining up, rooted in darkness, like a vine.
That's what you heard. If you're in the right mind
when it happens, it can come on you strong;
you might hear music passing on the wind,
or see a light where there wasn't one before."

"Well, how do you know if it amounts to anything?"

"You don't. It usually don't. It would take
a long time to ever know."

But that night
and other nights afterwards, up late,
there was a feeling in them—familiar
to them, but always startling in its strength—
like the thought, on a winter night,
of the lambing ewes dry-bedded and fed,
and the thought of the wild creatures warm
asleep in their nests, deep underground.

AWAKE AT NIGHT

Late in the night I pay
the unrest I owe
to the life that has never lived
and cannot live now.
What the world could be
is my good dream
and my agony when, dreaming it,
I lie awake and turn
and look into the dark.
I think of a luxury
in the sturdiness and grace
of necessary things, not
in frivolity. That would heal
the earth, and heal men.
But the end, too, is part
of the pattern, the last
labor of the heart:
to learn to lie still,
one with the earth
again, and let the world go.

PRAYERS AND SAYINGS OF
THE MAD FARMER

for James Baker Hall

I

It is presumptuous and irresponsible to pray for other people. A good man would pray only for himself—that he have as much good as he deserves, that he not receive more good or more evil than he deserves, that he bother nobody, that he not be bothered, that he want less. Praying thus for himself, he should prepare to live with the consequences.

II

At night make me one with the darkness.
In the morning make me one with the light.

III

If a man finds it necessary to eat garbage, he should resist the temptation to call it a delicacy.

IV

Don't pray for the rain to stop.
Pray for good luck fishing
when the river floods.

V

Don't own so much clutter that you will be relieved to see your house catch fire.

VI

Beware of the machinery of longevity. When a man's life is over the decent thing is for him to die. The forest does not withhold itself from death. What it gives up it takes back.

VII
Put your hands into the mire.
They will learn the kinship
of the shaped and the unshapen,
the living and the dead.

VIII
When I rise up
let me rise up joyful
like a bird.

When I fall
let me fall without regret
like a leaf.

IX
Sowing the seed,
my hand is one with the earth.

Wanting the seed to grow,
my mind is one with the light.

Hoeing the crop,
my hands are one with the rain.

Having cared for the plants,
my mind is one with the air.

Hungry and trusting,
my mind is one with the earth.

Eating the fruit,
my body is one with the earth.

X
Let my marriage by brought to the ground.
Let my love for this woman enrich the earth.

What is its happiness but preparing its place?
What is its monument but a rich field?

XI

By the excellence of his work the workman is a neighbor. By selling only what he would not despise to own the salesman is a neighbor. By selling what is good his character survives his market.

XII

Let me wake in the night
and hear it raining
and go back to sleep.

XIII

Don't worry and fret about the crops. After you have done all you can for them, let them stand in the weather on their own.

If the crop of any one year was all, a man would have to cut his throat every time it hailed.

But the *real* products of any year's work are the farmer's mind and the cropland itself.

If he raises a good crop at the cost of belittling himself and diminishing the ground, he has gained nothing. He will have to begin over again the next spring, worse off than before.

Let him receive the season's increment into his mind. Let him work it into the soil.

The finest growth that farmland can produce is a careful farmer.

Make the human race a better head. Make the world a better piece of ground.

THE SATISFACTIONS OF THE MAD FARMER

Growing weather; enough rain;
the cow's udder tight with milk;
the peach tree bent with its yield;
honey golden in the white comb;

the pastures deep in clover and grass,
enough, and more than enough;

the ground, new worked, moist
and yielding underfoot, the feet
comfortable in it as roots;

the early garden: potatoes, onions,
peas, lettuce, spinach, cabbage, carrots,
radishes, marking their straight rows
with green, before the trees are leafed;

raspberries ripe and heavy amid their foliage,
currants shining red in clusters amid their foliage,
strawberries red ripe with the white
flowers still on the vines—picked
with the dew on them, before breakfast;

grape clusters heavy under broad leaves,
powdery bloom on fruit black with sweetness
—an ancient delight, delighting;

the bodies of children, joyful
without dread of their spending,
surprised at nightfall to be weary;

the bodies of women in loose cotton,
cool and closed in the evenings
of summer, like contented houses;

the bodies of men, able in the heat
and sweat and weight and length
of the day's work, eager in their spending,
attending to nightfall, the bodies of women;

sleep after love, dreaming
white lilies blooming
coolly out of the flesh;

after sleep, enablement
to go on with work, morning a clear gift;

the maidenhood of the day,
cobwebs unbroken in the dewy grass;

the work of feeding and clothing and housing,
done with more than enough knowledge
and with more than enough love,
by those who do not have to be told;

any building well built, the rafters
firm to the walls, the walls firm,
the joists without give,
the proportions clear,
the fitting exact, even unseen,
bolts and hinges that turn home
without a jiggle;

any work worthy
of the day's maidenhood;

any man whose words
lead precisely to what exists,
who never stoops to persuasion;

the talk of friends, lightened and cleared
by all that can be assumed;

deer tracks in the wet path,
the deer sprung from them, gone on;

live streams, live shiftings
of the sun in the summer woods;

the great hollow-trunked beech,
a landmark I loved to return to,
its leaves gold-lit on the silver
branches in the fall: blown down
after a hundred years of standing,
a footbridge over the stream;

the quiet in the woods of a summer morning,
the voice of a pewee passing through it
like a tight silver wire;

a little clearing among cedars,
white clover and wild strawberries
beneath an opening to the sky
—heavenly, I thought it,
so perfect; had I foreseen it
I would have desired it
no less than it deserves;

fox tracks in snow, the impact
of lightness upon lightness,
unendingly silent.

What I know of spirit is astir
in the world. The god I have always expected
to appear at the woods' edge, beckoning,
I have always expected to be
a great relisher of this world, its good
grown immortal in his mind.

MEDITATION IN THE SPRING RAIN

In the April rain I climbed up to drink
of the live water leaping off the hill,
white over the rocks. Where the mossy root
of a sycamore cups the flow, I drank
and saw the branches feathered with green.
The thickets, I said, send up their praise
at dawn. Was that what I meant—I meant
my words to have the heft and grace, the flight
and weight of the very hill, its life
rising—or was it some old exultation
that abides with me? We'll not soon escape
the faith of our fathers—no more than
crazy old Mrs. Gaines, whom my grandmother
remembers standing balanced eighty years ago
atop a fence in Port Royal, Kentucky,
singing: "One Lord, one Faith, and one
Cornbread." They had a cage built for her
in a room, "nearly as big as the room, not
cramped up," and when she grew wild
they kept her there. But mostly she went free
in the town, and they allowed the children
to go for walks with her. She strayed once
beyond where they thought she went, was lost
to them, "and they had an awful time
finding her." For her, to be free
was only to be lost. What is it about her
that draws me on, so that my mind becomes a child
to follow after her? An old woman
when my grandmother was a girl, she must have seen
the virgin forest standing here, the amplitude
of our beginning, of which no speech
remains. Out of the town's lost history,
buried in minds long buried, she has come,
brought back by a memory near death. I see her

in her dusky clothes, hair uncombed, the children
following. I see her wandering, muttering
to herself as her way was, among these hills
half a century before my birth, in the silence
of such speech as I know. Dawn and twilight
and dawn again trembling in the leaves
over her, she tramped the raveling verges
of her time. It was a shadowy country
that she knew, holding a darkness that was past
and a darkness to come. The fleeting lights
tattered her churchly speech to mad song.
When her poor wandering head broke the confines
of all any of them knew, they put her in a cage.
But I am glad to know it was a commodious cage,
not cramped up. And I am glad to know
that other times the town left her free
to be as she was in it, and to go her way.
May it abide a poet with as much grace!
For I too am perhaps a little mad,
standing here wet in the drizzle, listening
to the clashing syllables of the water. Surely
there is a great Word being put together here.
I begin to hear it gather in the opening
of the flowers and the leafing-out of the trees,
in the growth of bird nests in the crotches
of the branches, in the settling of the dead
leaves into the ground, in the whittling
of beetle and grub, in my thoughts
moving in the hill's flesh. Coming here,
I crossed a place where a stream flows
underground, and the sounds of the hidden water
and the water come to light braided in my ear.
I think the maker is here, creating his hill
as it will be, out of what it was.
The thickets, I say, send up their praise
at dawn! One Lord, one Faith, and one Cornbread

forever! But hush. Wait. Be as still
as the dead and the unborn in whose silence
that old one walked, muttering and singing,
followed by the children.

                    For a time there
I turned away from the words I knew, and was lost.
For a time I was lost and free, speechless
in the multitudinous assembling of his Word.

❈❈❈❈❈❈

THE GRANDMOTHER

Better born than married, misled,
in the heavy summers of the river bottom
and the long winters cut off by snow
she would crave gentle dainty things,
"a pretty little cookie or a cup of tea,"
but spent her days over a wood stove
cooking cornbread, kettles of jowl and beans
for the heavy, hungry, hard-handed
men she had married and mothered, bent
past unbending by her days of labor
that love had led her to. They had to break her
before she would lie down in her coffin.

THE HERON

While the summer's growth kept me
anxious in planted rows, I forgot the river
where it flowed, faithful to its way,
beneath the slope where my household
has taken its laborious stand.
I could not reach it even in dreams.
But one morning at the summer's end
I remember it again, as though its being
lifts into mind in undeniable flood,
and I carry my boat down through the fog,
over the rocks, and set out.
I go easy and silent, and the warblers
appear among the leaves of the willows,
their flight like gold thread
quick in the live tapestry of the leaves.
And I go on until I see, crouched
on a dead branch sticking out of the water,
a heron—so still that I believe
he is a bit of drift hung dead above the water.
And then I see the articulation of feather
and living eye, a brilliance I receive
beyond my power to make, as he
receives in his great patience
the river's providence. And then I see
that I am seen. Still as I keep,
I might be a tree for all the fear he shows.
Suddenly I know I have passed across
to a shore where I do not live.

SEPTEMBER 2, 1969

In the evening there were flocks of nighthawks
passing southward over the valley. The tall
sunflowers stood, burning on their stalks
to cold seed, by the river. And high
up the birds rose into sight against the darkening
clouds. They tossed themselves among the fading
landscapes of the sky like rags, as in
abandonment to the summons their blood knew.
And in my mind, where had stood a garden
straining to the light, there grew
an acceptance of decline. Having worked,
I would sleep, my leaves all dissolved in flight.

THE FARMER, SPEAKING OF MONUMENTS

Always, on their generation's breaking wave,
men think to be immortal in the world,
as though to leap from water and stand
in air were simple for a man. But the farmer
knows no work or act of his can keep him
here. He remains in what he serves
by vanishing in it, becoming what he never was.
He will not be immortal in words.
All his sentences serve an art of the commonplace,
to open the body of a woman or a field
to take him in. His words all turn
to leaves, answering the sun with mute
quick reflections. Leaving their seed, his hands
have had a million graves, from which wonders
rose, bearing him no likeness. At summer's
height he is surrounded by green, his
doing, standing for him, awake and orderly.
In autumn, all his monuments fall.

THE SORREL FILLY

The songs of small birds fade away
into the bushes after sundown,
the air dry, sweet with goldenrod.
Beside the path, suddenly, bright asters
flare in the dusk. The aged voices
of a few crickets thread the silence.
It is a quiet I love, though my life
too often drives me through it deaf.
Busy with costs and losses, I waste
the time I have to be here—a time
blessed beyond my deserts, as I know,
if only I would keep aware. The leaves
rest in the air, perfectly still.
I would like them to rest in my mind
as still, as simply spaced. As I approach,
the sorrel filly looks up from her grazing,
poised there, light on the slope
as a young apple tree. A week ago
I took her away to sell, and failed
to get my price, and brought her home
again. Now in the quiet I stand
and look at her a long time, glad
to have recovered what is lost
in the exchange of something for money.

TO THE UNSEEABLE ANIMAL

My daughter: *"I hope there's an animal
somewhere that nobody has ever seen.
And I hope nobody ever sees it."*

Being, whose flesh dissolves
at our glance, knower
of the secret sums and measures,
you are always here,
dwelling in the oldest sycamores,
visiting the faithful springs
when they are dark and the foxes
have crept to their edges.
I have come upon pools
in streams, places overgrown
with the woods' shadow,
where I knew you had rested,
watching the little fish
hang still in the flow;
as I approached they seemed
particles of your clear mind
disappearing among the rocks.
I have waked deep in the woods
in the early morning, sure
that while I slept
your gaze passed over me.
That we do not know you
is your perfection
and our hope. The darkness
keeps us near you.

THE COUNTRY OF MARRIAGE

(1973)

*. . . Except a corn of wheat fall into the
ground and die, it abideth alone . . .*

JOHN 12:24

THE OLD ELM TREE BY THE RIVER

Shrugging in the flight of its leaves,
it is dying. Death is slowly
standing up in its trunk and branches
like a camouflaged hunter. In the night
I am wakened by one of its branches
crashing down, heavy as a wall, and then
lie sleepless, the world changed.
That is a life I know the country by.
Mine is a life I know the country by.
Willing to live and die, we stand here,
timely and at home, neighborly as two men.
Our place is changing in us as we stand,
and we hold up the weight that will bring us down.
In us the land enacts its history.
When we stood it was beneath us, and was
the strength by which we held to it
and stood, the daylight over it
a mighty blessing we cannot bear for long.

POEM

Willing to die,
you give up
your will, keep still
until, moved
by what moves
all else, you move.

❁❁❁❁❁❁❁❁❁

BREAKING

Did I believe I had a clear mind?
It was like the water of a river
flowing shallow over the ice. And now
that the rising water has broken
the ice, I see that what I thought
was the light is part of the dark.

THE COUNTRY OF MARRIAGE

1.

I dream of you walking at night along the streams
of the country of my birth, warm blooms and the nightsongs
of birds opening around you as you walk.
You are holding in your body the dark seed of my sleep.

2.

This comes after silence. Was it something I said
that bound me to you, some mere promise
or, worse, the fear of loneliness and death?
A man lost in the woods in the dark, I stood
still and said nothing. And then there rose in me,
like the earth's empowering brew rising
in root and branch, the words of a dream of you
I did not know I had dreamed. I was a wanderer
who feels the solace of his native land
under his feet again and moving in his blood.
I went on, blind and faithful. Where I stepped
my track was there to steady me. It was no abyss
that lay before me, but only the level ground.

3.

Sometimes our life reminds me
of a forest in which there is a graceful clearing
and in that opening a house,
an orchard and garden,
comfortable shades, and flowers
red and yellow in the sun, a pattern
made in the light for the light to return to.
The forest is mostly dark, its ways
to be made anew day after day, the dark
richer than the light and more blessed,
provided we stay brave
enough to keep on going in.

4.

How many times have I come to you out of my head
with joy, if ever a man was,
for to approach you I have given up the light
and all directions. I come to you
lost, wholly trusting as a man who goes
into the forest unarmed. It is as though I descend
slowly earthward out of the air. I rest in peace
in you, when I arrive at last.

5.

Our bond is no little economy based on the exchange
of my love and work for yours, so much for so much
of an expendable fund. We don't know what its limits are—
that puts it in the dark. We are more together
than we know, how else could we keep on discovering
we are more together than we thought?
You are the known way leading always to the unknown,
and you are the known place to which the unknown is always
leading me back. More blessed in you than I know,
I possess nothing worthy to give you, nothing
not belittled by my saying that I possess it.
Even an hour of love is a moral predicament, a blessing
a man may be hard up to be worthy of. He can only
accept it, as a plant accepts from all the bounty of the light
enough to live, and then accepts the dark,
passing unencumbered back to the earth, as I
have fallen time and again from the great strength
of my desire, helpless, into your arms.

6.

What I am learning to give you is my death
to set you free of me, and me from myself
into the dark and the new light. Like the water
of a deep stream, love is always too much. We
did not make it. Though we drink till we burst

we cannot have it all, or want it all.
In its abundance it survives our thirst.
In the evening we come down to the shore
to drink our fill, and sleep, while it
flows through the regions of the dark.
It does not hold us, except we keep returning
to its rich waters thirsty. We enter,
willing to die, into the commonwealth of its joy.

7.

I give you what is unbounded, passing from dark to dark,
containing darkness: a night of rain, an early morning.
I give you the life I have let live for love of you:
a clump of orange-blooming weeds beside the road,
the young orchard waiting in the snow, our own life
that we have planted in this ground, as I
have planted mine in you. I give you my love for all
beautiful and honest women that you gather to yourself
again and again, and satisfy—and this poem,
no more mine than any man's who has loved a woman.

❀❦❀❦❀❦❀❦❀

PRAYER AFTER EATING

I have taken in the light
that quickened eye and leaf.
May my brain be bright with praise
of what I eat, in the brief blaze
of motion and of thought.
May I be worthy of my meat.

HER FIRST CALF

Her fate seizes her and brings her
down. She is heavy with it. It
wrings her. The great weight
is heaved out of her. It eases.
She moves into what she has become,
sure in her fate now
as a fish free in the current.
She turns to the calf who has broken
out of the womb's water and its veil.
He breathes. She licks his wet hair.
He gathers his legs under him
and rises. He stands, and his legs
wobble. After the months
of his pursuit of her, now
they meet face to face.
From the beginnings of the world
his arrival and her welcome
have been prepared. They have always
known each other.

KENTUCKY RIVER JUNCTION

to Ken Kesey & Ken Babbs

Clumsy at first, fitting together
the years we have been apart,
and the ways.

But as the night
passed and the day came, the first
fine morning of April,

it came clear:
the world that has tried us
and showed us its joy

was our bond
when we said nothing.
And we allowed it to be

with us, the new green
shining.

✦

Our lives, half gone,
stay full of laughter.

Free-hearted men
have the world for words.

Though we have been
apart, we have been together.

✦

Trying to sleep, I cannot
take my mind away.
The bright day

shines in my head
like a coin
on the bed of a stream.

☙

You left
your welcome.

MANIFESTO: THE MAD FARMER
LIBERATION FRONT

Love the quick profit, the annual raise,
vacation with pay. Want more
of everything ready-made. Be afraid
to know your neighbors and to die.
And you will have a window in your head.
Not even your future will be a mystery
any more. Your mind will be punched in a card
and shut away in a little drawer.
When they want you to buy something
they will call you. When they want you
to die for profit they will let you know.
So, friends, every day do something
that won't compute. Love the Lord.
Love the world. Work for nothing.
Take all that you have and be poor.
Love somebody who does not deserve it.
Denounce the government and embrace
the flag. Hope to live in that free
republic for which it stands.
Give your approval to all you cannot
understand. Praise ignorance, for what man
has not encountered he has not destroyed.
Ask the questions that have no answers.
Invest in the millennium. Plant sequoias.
Say that your main crop is the forest
that you did not plant,
that you will not live to harvest.
Say that the leaves are harvested
when they have rotted into the mold.
Call that profit. Prophesy such returns.
Put your faith in the two inches of humus
that will build under the trees
every thousand years.

Listen to carrion—put your ear
close, and hear the faint chattering
of the songs that are to come.
Expect the end of the world. Laugh.
Laughter is immeasurable. Be joyful
though you have considered all the facts.
So long as women do not go cheap
for power, please women more than men.
Ask yourself: Will this satisfy
a woman satisfied to bear a child?
Will this disturb the sleep
of a woman near to giving birth?
Go with your love to the fields.
Lie easy in the shade. Rest your head
in her lap. Swear allegiance
to what is nighest your thoughts.
As soon as the generals and the politicos
can predict the motions of your mind,
lose it. Leave it as a sign
to mark the false trail, the way
you didn't go. Be like the fox
who makes more tracks than necessary,
some in the wrong direction.
Practice resurrection.

A MARRIAGE, AN ELEGY

They lived long, and were faithful
to the good in each other.
They suffered as their faith required.
Now their union is consummate
in earth, and the earth
is their communion. They enter
the serene gravity of the rain,
the hill's passage to the sea.
After long striving, perfect ease.

❁❁❁❁❁❁

THE ARRIVAL

Like a tide it comes in,
wave after wave of foliage and fruit,
the nurtured and the wild,
out of the light to this shore.
In its extravagance we shape
the strenuous outline of enough.

A SONG SPARROW SINGING IN THE FALL

Somehow it has all
added up to song—
earth, air, rain and light,
the labor and the heat,
the mortality of the young.
I will go free of other
singing, I will go
into the silence
of my songs, to hear
this song clearly.

THE MAD FARMER MANIFESTO:
THE FIRST AMENDMENT

1.

". . . it is not too soon to provide by every
possible means that as few as possible shall be
without a little portion of land. The small
landholders are the most precious part of a state."
  Jefferson, to Reverend James Madison, October 28, 1785.

That is the glimmering vein
of our sanity, dividing from us
from the start: land under us
to steady us when we stood,
free men in the great communion
of the free. The vision keeps
lighting in my mind, a window
on the horizon in the dark.

2.

To be sane in a mad time
is bad for the brain, worse
for the heart. The world
is a holy vision, had we clarity
to see it—a clarity that men
depend on men to make.

3.

It is *ignorant* money I declare
myself free from, money fat
and dreaming in its sums, driving
us into the streets of absence,
stranding the pasture trees
in the deserted language of banks.

4.

And I declare myself free
from ignorant love. You easy lovers
and forgivers of mankind, stand back!
I will love you at a distance,
and not because you deserve it.
My love must be discriminate
or fail to bear its weight.

PLANTING TREES

In the mating of trees,
the pollen grain entering invisible
the domed room of the winds, survives
the ghost of the old forest
that stood here when we came. The ground
invites it, and it will not be gone.
I become the familiar of that ghost
and its ally, carrying in a bucket
twenty trees smaller than weeds,
and I plant them along the way
of the departure of the ancient host.
I return to the ground its original music.
It will rise out of the horizon
of the grass, and over the heads
of the weeds, and it will rise over
the horizon of men's heads. As I age
in the world it will rise and spread,
and be for this place horizon
and orison, the voice of its winds.
I have made myself a dream to dream
of its rising, that has gentled my nights.
Let me desire and wish well the life
these trees may live when I
no longer rise in the mornings
to be pleased by the green of them
shining, and their shadows on the ground,
and the sound of the wind in them.

THE WILD GEESE

Horseback on Sunday morning,
harvest over, we taste persimmon
and wild grape, sharp sweet
of summer's end. In time's maze
over the fall fields, we name names
that went west from here, names
that rest on graves. We open
a persimmon seed to find the tree
that stands in promise,
pale, in the seed's marrow.
Geese appear high over us,
pass, and the sky closes. Abandon,
as in love or sleep, holds
them to their way, clear,
in the ancient faith: what we need
is here. And we pray, not
for new earth or heaven, but to be
quiet in heart, and in eye
clear. What we need is here.

THE SILENCE

Though the air is full of singing
my head is loud
with the labor of words.

Though the season is rich
with fruit, my tongue
hungers for the sweet of speech.

Though the beech is golden
I cannot stand beside it
mute, but must say

"It is golden," while the leaves
stir and fall with a sound
that is not a name.

It is in the silence
that my hope is, and my aim.
A song whose lines

I cannot make or sing
sounds men's silence
like a root. Let me say

and not mourn: the world
lives in the death of speech
and sings there.

ANGER AGAINST BEASTS

The hook of adrenaline shoves
into the blood. Man's will,
long schooled to kill or have
its way, would drive the beast
against nature, transcend
the impossible in simple fury.
The blow falls like a dead seed.
It is defeat, for beasts
do not pardon, but heal or die
in the absence of the past.
The blow survives in the man.
His triumph is a wound. Spent,
he must wait the slow
unalterable forgiveness of time.

AT A COUNTRY FUNERAL

Now the old ways that have brought us
farther than we remember sink out of sight
as under the treading of many strangers
ignorant of landmarks. Only once in a while
they are cast clear again upon the mind
as at a country funeral where, amid the soft
lights and hothouse flowers, the expensive
solemnity of experts, notes of a polite musician,
persist the usages of old neighborhood.
Friends and kinsmen come and stand and speak,
knowing the extremity they have come to,
one of the their own bearing to the earth the last
of his light, his darkness the sun's definitive mark.
They stand and think as they stood and thought
when even the gods were different.
And the organ music, though decorous
as for somebody else's grief, has its source
in the outcry of pain and hope in log churches,
and on naked hillsides by the open grave,
eastward in mountain passes, in tidelands,
and across the sea. How long a time?
Rock of Ages, cleft for me, let my hide my
self in Thee. They came, once in time,
in simple loyalty to their dead, and returned
to the world. The fields and the work
remained to be returned to. Now the entrance
of one of the old ones into the Rock
too often means a lifework perished from the land
without inheritor, and the field goes wild
and the house sits and stares. Or it passes
at cash value into the hands of strangers.
Now the old dead wait in the open coffin
for the blood kin to gather, come home
for one last time, to hear old men

whose tongues bear an essential topography
speak memories doomed to die.
But our memory of ourselves, hard earned,
is one of the land's seeds, as a seed
is the memory of the life of its kind in its place,
to pass on into life the knowledge
of what has died. What we owe the future
is not a new start, for we can only begin
with what has happened. We owe the future
the past, the long knowledge
that is the potency of time to come.
That makes of a man's grave a rich furrow.
The community of knowing in common is the seed
of our life in this place. There is not only
no better possibility, there is no
other, except for chaos and darkness,
the terrible ground of the only possible
new start. And so as the old die and the young
depart, where shall a man go who keeps
the memories of the dead, except home
again, as one would go back after a burial,
faithful to the fields, lest the dead die
a second and more final death.

THE RECOGNITION

You put on my clothes
and it was as though
we met some other place
and I looked and knew
you. This is what we keep
going through, the lyrical
changes, the strangeness
in which I know again
what I have known before.

PLANTING CROCUSES

1.

I made an opening
to reach through blind
into time, through
sleep and silence, to new
heat, a new rising,
a yellow flower opening
in the sound of bees.

2.

Deathly was the giving
of that possibility
to a motion of the world
that would bring it
out, bright, in time.

3.

My mind pressing in
through the earth's
dark motion toward
bloom, I thought of you,
glad there is no escape.
It is this we will be
turning and re-
turning to.

PRAISE

1.

Don't think of it.
Vanity is absence.
Be here. Here
is the root and stem
unappraisable
on whose life
your life depends

2.

Be here
like the water
of the hill
that fills each
opening it
comes to, to leave
with a sound
that is a part
of local speech.

THE GATHERING

At my age my father
held me on his arm
like a hooded bird,
and his father held him so.
Now I grow into brotherhood
with my father as he
with his has grown,
time teaching me
his thoughts in my own.
Now he speaks in me
as when I knew him first,
as his father spoke
in him when he had come
to thirst for the life
of a young son. My son
will know me in himself
when his son sits hooded on
his arm and I have grown
to be brother to all
my fathers, memory
speaking to knowledge,
finally, in my bones.

A HOMECOMING

One faith is bondage. Two
are free. In the trust
of old love, cultivation shows
a dark graceful wilderness
at its heart. Wild
in that wilderness, we roam
the distances of our faith,
safe beyond the bounds
of what we know. O love,
open. Show me
my country. Take me home.

❁❀❁❀❁❀❁❀❁

THE MAD FARMER'S LOVE SONG

O when the world's at peace
and every man is free
then will I go down unto my love.

O and I may go down
several times before that.

TESTAMENT

And now to the Abbyss I pass
Of that unfathomable Grass...

1.

Dear relatives and friends, when my last breath
Grows large and free in air, don't call it death—
A word to enrich the undertaker and inspire
His surly art of imitating life; conspire
Against him. Say that my body cannot now
Be improved upon; it has no fault to show
To the sly cosmetician. Say that my flesh
Has a perfection in compliance with the grass
Truer than any it could have striven for.
You will recognize the earth in me, as before
I wished to know it in myself: my earth
That has been my care and faithful charge from birth,
And toward which all my sorrows were surely bound,
And all my hopes. Say that I have found
A good solution, and am on my way
To the roots. And say I have left my native clay
At last, to be a traveler; that too will be so.
Traveler to where? Say you don't know.

2.

But do not let your ignorance
Of my spirit's whereabouts dismay
You, or overwhelm your thoughts.
Be careful not to say

Anything too final. Whatever
Is unsure is possible, and life is bigger
Than flesh. Beyond reach of thought
Let imagination figure

Your hope. That will be generous
To me and to yourselves. Why settle
For some know-it-all's despair
When the dead may dance to the fiddle

Hereafter, for all anybody knows?
And remember that the Heavenly soil
Need not be too rich to please
One who was happy in Port Royal.

I may be already heading back,
A new and better man, toward
That town. The thought's unreasonable,
But so is life, thank the Lord!

3.

So treat me, even dead,
As a man who has a place
To go, and something to do
Don't muck up my face

With wax and powder and rouge
As one would prettify
An unalterable fact
To give bitterness the lie.

Admit the native earth
My body is and will be,
Admit its freedom and
Its changeability.

Dress me in the clothes
I wore in the day's round.
Lay me in a wooden box.
Put the box in the ground.

4.

Beneath this stone a Berry is planted
In his home land, as he wanted.

He has come to the gathering of his kin,
Among whom some were worthy men,

Farmers mostly, who lived by hand,
But one was a cobbler from Ireland,

Another played the eternal fool
By riding on a circus mule

To be remembered in grateful laughter
Longer than the rest. After

Doing what they had to do
They are at ease here. Let all of you

Who yet for pain find force and voice
Look on their peace, and rejoice.

THE CLEAR DAYS

for Allen Tate

The dogs of indecision
Cross and cross the field of vision.

A cloud, a buzzing fly
Distract the lover's eye.

Until the heart has found
Its native piece of ground

The day withholds its light,
The eye must stray unlit.

The ground's the body's bride,
Who will not be denied.

Not until all is given
Comes the thought of heaven.

When the mind's an empty room
The clear days come.

SONG

I tell my love in rhyme
In a sentence that must end,
A measurable dividend,
To hold her time against time.

I praise her honest eyes
That keep their beauty clear.
I have nothing to fear
From her, though the world lies,

If I don't lie. Though the hill
Of winter rise, a silent ark,
Our covenant with the dark,
We will speak on until

The flowers fall, and the birds
With their bright songs depart.
Then we will go without art,
Without measure, or words.

POEM FOR J.

What she made in her body is broken.
Now she has begun to bear it again.
In the house of her son's death
his life is shining in the windows,
for she has elected to bear him again.
She did not bear him for death,
and she does not. She has taken back
into her body the seed, bitter
and joyous, of the life of a man.

In the house of the dead the windows shine
with life. She mourns, for his life was good.
She is not afraid. She is like a field
where the corn is planted, and like the rain
that waters the field, and like the young corn.
In her sorrow she renews life, in her grief
she prepares the return of joy.

She did not bear him for death, and she does not.
There was a life that went out of her to live
on its own, divided, and now she has taken it back.
She is alight with the sudden new life of death.
Perhaps it is the brightness of the dead one
being born again. Perhaps she is planting him,
like corn, in the living and in the earth.
She has taken back into her flesh,
and made light, the dark seed of her pain.

THE LONG HUNTER

Passed through the dark wall,
set foot in the unknown track,
paths locked in the minds of beasts
and in strange tongues. Footfall
led him where he did not know.
There was a dark country where
only blind trust could go.
Some joyous animal paced the woods
ahead of him and filled the air
with steepling song to make a way.
Step by step the darkness bore
the light. The shadow opened
like a pod, and from the height
he saw a place green as welcome
on whose still water the sky lay white.

AN ANNIVERSARY

What we have been becomes
The country where we are.
Spring goes, summer comes,
And in the heat, as one year
Or a thousand years before,
The fields and woods prepare
The burden of their seed
Out of time's wound, the old
Richness of the fall. Their deed
Is renewal. In the household
Of the woods the past
Is always healing in the light,
The high shiftings of the air.
It stands upon its yield
And thrives. Nothing is lost.
What yields, though in despair,
Opens and rises in the night.
Love binds us to this term
With its yes that is crying
In our marrow to confirm
Life that only lives by dying.
Lovers live by the moon
Whose dark and light are one,
Changing without rest.
The root struts from the seed
In the earth's dark—harvest
And feast at the edge of sleep.
Darkened, we are carried
Out of need, deep
In the country we have married.

5/29/72

CLEARING

(1977)

For Dan Wickenden

What has been spoiled through man's fault can be
made good again through man's work. *I Ching*

✦

Handles are shining where my life has passed.
My fields and walls are aching
in my shoulders. My subjects are my objects:
house, barn, beast, hill, and tree.
Reader, make no mistake. The meanings
of these must balance against their weight.

HISTORY

For Wallace Stegner

1.

The crops were made, the leaves
were down, three frosts had lain
upon the broad stone
step beneath the door;
as I walked away
the houses were shut, quiet
under their drifting smokes,
the women stooped at the hearths.
Beyond the farthest tracks
of any domestic beast
my way led me, into
a place for which I knew
no names. I went by paths
that bespoke intelligence
and memory I did not know.
Noonday held sounds of moving
water, moving air, enormous
stillness of old trees.
Though I was weary and alone,
song was near me then,
wordless and gay as a deer
lightly stepping. Learning
the landmarks and the ways
of that land, so I might
go back, if I wanted to,
my mind grew new, and lost
the backward way. I stood

at last, long hunter and child,
where this valley opened,
a word I seemed to know
though I had not heard it.
Behind me, along the crooks
and slants of my approach,
a low song sang itself,
as patient as the light.
On the valley floor the woods
grew rich: great poplars,
beeches, sycamores,
walnuts, sweet gums, lindens,
oaks. They stood apart
and open, the winter light
at rest among them. Yes,
and as I came down
I heard a little stream
pouring into the river.

2.

Since then I have arrived here
many times. I have come
on foot, on horseback, by boat,
and by machine—by earth,
water, air, and fire.
I came with axe and rifle.
I came with a sharp eye
and the price of land. I came
in bondage, and I came
in freedom not worth the name.
From the high outlook
of that first day I have come
down two hundred years
across the worked and wasted
slopes, by eroding tracks
of the joyless horsepower of greed.

Through my history's despite
and ruin, I have come
to its remainder, and here
have made the beginning
of a farm intended to become
my art of being here.
By it I would instruct
my wants: they should belong
to each other and to this place.
Until my song comes here
to learn its words, my art
is but the hope of song.

    3.

All the lives this place
has had, I have. I eat
my history day by day.
Bird, butterfly, and flower
pass through the seasons of
my flesh. I dine and thrive
on offal and old stone,
and am combined within
the story of the ground.
By this earth's life, I have
its greed and innocence,
its violence, its peace.
Now let me feed my song
upon the life that is here
that is the life that is gone.
This blood has turned to dust
and liquefied again in stem
and vein ten thousand times.
Let what is in the flesh,
O Muse, be brought to mind.

WHERE

The field mouse flickers
once upon his shadow,
is gone. The watcher is left
in all silence, as after
thunder, or threat. And then
in the top of the sycamore
the redbird opens again
his clear song: *Even
so. Even so.*
Divided by little songs
these silences keep folding
back upon themselves
like long cloths put away.
They are all of the one
silence that precedes
and follows us. Too much
has fallen silent here.
There are names that rest
as silent on their stone
as fossils in creek ledges.
There are those who sleep
in graves no one remembers;
there is no language here,
now, to speak their names.

✝

Too much of our history
will seem to have taken place
in the halls of capitals,
where the accusers have
mostly been guilty, and so
have borne witness to nothing.
Whole lives of work are buried

under leaves of thickets,
hands fallen from helves.
What was memory is dust
now, and many a story
told in shade or by the fire
is gone with the old light.
On the courthouse shelves
the facts lie mute
upon their pages, useless
nearly as the old boundary
marks — "Beginning on
the bank of the Kentucky River
at the mouth of Cane Run
at a hackberry" (1865) —
lost in the silence of
old days and voices. And yet
the land and the mind
bear the marks of a history
that they do not record.

✦

The mind still hungers
for its earth, its bounded
and open space, the term
of its final assent. It keeps
the vision of an independent
modest abundance. It dreams
of cellar and pantry filled,
the source well husbanded.
And yet it learns care
reluctantly, and late.
It suffers plaintively from
its obligations. Long
attention to detail
is a cross it bears only

by congratulating itself.
It would like to hurry up
and get more than it needs
of several pleasant things.
It dreads all the labors
of common decency.
It recalls, with disquieting
sympathy, the motto
of a locally renowned
and long dead kinsman: "Never
set up when you can lay down."

†

The land bears the scars
of minds whose history
was imprinted by no example
of a forebearing mind, corrected,
beloved. A mind cast loose
in whim and greed makes
nature its mirror, and the garden
falls with the man. Great trees
once crowded this bottomland,
so thick that when they were felled
a boy could walk a mile
along their trunks and never
set foot to ground. Where
that forest stood, the fields
grew fine crops of hay:
men tied the timothy heads
together across their horses'
withers; the mountains upstream
were wooded then, and the river
in flood renewed its fields
like the Nile. Given
a live, husbandly tradition,

that abundance might
have lasted. It did not.
One lifetime of our history
ruined it. The slopes
of the watershed were stripped
of trees. The black topsoil
washed away in the tracks
of logger and plowman.
The creeks, that once ran clear
after the heaviest rains,
ran muddy, dried in summer.
From year to year watching
from his porch, my grandfather
saw a barn roof slowly
come into sight above
a neighboring ridge as plows
and rains wore down the hill.
This little has been remembered.
For the rest, one must go
and ponder in the silence
of documents, or decipher
on the land itself the healed
gullies and the unhealed,
the careless furrows drawn
over slopes too steep to plow
where the scrub growth
stands in vision's failure now.

✦

Such a mind is as much
a predicament as such
a place. And yet a knowledge
is here that tenses the throat
as for song: the inheritance
of the ones, alive or once

alive, who stand behind
the ones I have imagined,
who took into their minds
the troubles of this place,
blights of love and race,
but saw a good fate here
and willingly paid its cost,
kept it the best they could,
thought of its good,
and mourned the good they lost.

THE CLEARING

For Hayden Carruth

1.

Through elm, buckeye, thorn,
box elder, redbud, whitehaw,
locust thicket, all trees
that follow man's neglect,
through snarls and veils
of honeysuckle, tangles
of grape and bittersweet,
sing, steel, the hard song
of vision cutting in.

2.

Vision must have severity
at its edge:

        against neglect,
bushes grown over the pastures,
vines riding down
the fences, the cistern broken;

against the false vision
of the farm dismembered,
sold in pieces on the condition
of the buyer's ignorance,
a disorderly town
of "houses in the country"
inhabited by strangers;

against indifference, the tracks
of the bulldozer running
to gullies;

against weariness,
the dread of too much to do,
the wish to make desire
easy, the thought of rest.

3.
"We don't bother nobody,
and we don't want nobody
to bother us," the old woman
declared fiercely
over the fence. She stood
in strange paradise:
a shack built in the blast
of sun on the riverbank,
a place under the threat of flood,
bought ignorantly, not
to be bothered. And that
is what has come of it,
"the frontier spirit," lost
in the cities, returning now
to be lost in the country,
obscure desire floating
like a cloud upon vision:
to be free of labor,
the predicament of other lives,
not to be bothered.

4.
Vision reaches the ground
under sumac and thorn,
under the honeysuckle,
and begins its rise.
It sees clear pasture,
clover and grass, on the worn
hillside going back
to woods, good cropland

in the bottom gone to weeds.
Through time, labor, the fret
of effort, it sees
cattle on the green slope
adrift in the daily current
of hunger. And vision
moderates the saw blade,
the intelligence
and mercy of that power.
Against nature, nature
will serve well enough
a man who does not ask too much.
We leave the walnut trees,
graces of the ground
flourishing in the air.

5.

A man who does not ask too much
becomes the promise of his land.

His marriage married
to his place, he waits

and does not stray. He takes thought
for the return of the dead

to the ground that they may come
to their last avail,

for the rain
that it stay long in reach of roots,

for roots
that they bind the living

to the dead, for sleep
that it bring breath through the dark,

for love in whose keeping
bloom comes to light.

Singularity made him great
in his sight.

This union makes him small,
a part of what he would keep.

6.

As the vision of labor grows
grows the vision of rest.
Weariness is work's shadow.
Labor is no preparation
but takes life as it goes
and casts upon it
death's shadow, which
enough weariness may welcome.
The body's death rises
over its daily labor,
a tree to rest beneath.
But work clarifies
the vision of rest. In rest
the vision of rest is lost.

⸙

The farm is the proper destiny,
here now and to come.
Leave the body to die
in its time, in the final dignity
that knows no loss in the fallen
high horse of the bones.

7.

In the predicament of other lives
we become mothers of calves,
teaching them, against nature,
to suck a bucket's valved nipple,
caring for them like life
itself to make them complete
animals, independent
of the tit. Fidelity
reaches through the night
to the triumph of their lives,
bawling in the cold barn before
daylight—to become, eaten,
the triumph of other lives
perhaps not worthy of them,
eaters who will recognize
only their own lives
in their daily meat.

✦

But no matter. Life
must be served. Wake up,
leave the bed, dress
in the cold room, go under
stars to the barn, come
to the greetings of hunger,
the breath a pale awning
in the dark. Feed
the lives that feed
lives.

✦

When one sickens
do not let him die. Hold out

against the simple flesh
that would let its life go
in the cold night. While he lives
a thought belongs to him
that will not rest. And then
accept the relief of death.
Drag the heedless carcass
out of the stall, fling it
in the bushes, let it
lie. Hunger will find it,
the bones divide by stealth,
the black head with its star
drift into the hill.

8.

Streets, guns, machines,
quicker fortunes, quicker deaths
bear down on these
hills whose winter trees
keep like memories
the nests of birds. The arrival
may be complete in my time,
and I will see the end
of names. The history
of lives will end then,
the building and wearing away
of earth and flesh will end,
and the history of numbers
will begin. Then why clear
yet again an old farm
scarred by the lack of sight
that scars our souls?
The struggle is on, no
mistake, and I take
the side of life's history
against the coming of numbers.

Make clear what was overgrown.
Cut the brush, drag it
through sumac and briars, pile it,
clear the old fence rows,
the trash dump, stop
the washes, mend the galls,
fence and sow the fields,
bring cattle back to graze
the slopes, bring crops back
to the bottomland. Here
where the time of rain is kept
take what is half ruined
and make it clear, put it
back in mind.

9.

February. A cloudy day
foretelling spring by its warmth
though snow will follow.
You are at work in the worn field
returning now to thought.
The sorrel mare eager
to the burden, you are dragging
cut brush to the pile,
moving in ancestral motions
of axe-stroke, bending
to log chain and trace, speaking
immemorial bidding and praise
to the mare's fine ears.
And you pause to rest
in the quiet day while the mare's
sweated flanks steam.
You stand in a clearing whose cost
you know in tendon and bone.
A kingfisher utters
his harsh cry, rising

from the leafless river.
Again, again, the old
is newly come.

10.

We pile the brush high,
a pyre of cut trees,
not to burn as the way
once was, but to rot and cover
an old scar of the ground.

The dead elm, its stump
and great trunk too heavy to move,
we give to the riddance of fire.
Two days, two nights
it burns, white ash falling
from it light as snow.

It goes into the air.
What bore the wind
the wind will bear.

11.

An evening comes
when we finish work and go,
stumblers under the folding sky,
the field clear behind us.

WORK SONG

1. *A Lineage*

By the fall of years I learn how it has been
With Jack Beechum, Mat Feltner, Elton Penn,

And their kind, men made for their fields.
I see them stand their ground, bear their yields,

Swaying in all weathers in their long rows,
In the dance that fleshes desire and then goes

Down with the light. They have gone as they came,
And they go. They go by a kind of will. They claim

In the brevity of their strength an ancient joy.
"Make me know it! Hand it to me, boy!"

2. *A Vision*

If we will have the wisdom to survive,
to stand like slow-growing trees
on a ruined place, renewing, enriching it,
if we will make our seasons welcome here,
asking not too much of earth or heaven,
then a long time after we are dead
the lives our lives prepare will live
here, their houses strongly placed
upon the valley sides, fields and gardens
rich in the windows. The river will run
clear, as we will never know it,
and over it, birdsong like a canopy.
On the levels of the hills will be
green meadows, stock bells in noon shade.
On the steeps where greed and ignorance cut down
the old forest, an old forest will stand,
its rich leaf-fall drifting on its roots.

The veins of forgotten springs will have opened.
Families will be singing in the fields.
In their voices they will hear a music
risen out of the ground. They will take
nothing from the ground they will not return,
whatever the grief at parting. Memory,
native to this valley, will spread over it
like a grove, and memory will grow
into legend, legend into song, song
into sacrament. The abundance of this place,
the songs of its people and its birds,
will be health and wisdom and indwelling
light. This is no paradisal dream.
Its hardship is its possibility.

3. A Beginning

October's completing light falls
on the unfinished patterns of my year.
The sun is yellow in a smudge
of public lies we no longer try
to believe. Speech finally drives us
to silence. Power has weakened us.
Comfort wakens us in fear. We are
a people who must decline or perish.
I have let my mind at last bend down
where human vision begins its rise
in the dark of seeds, wombs of beasts.
It has carried my hands to roots
and foundings, to the mute urging
that in human care clears the field
and turns it green. It reaches
the silence at the tongue's root
in which speech begins. In early mist
I walk in these reopening fields
as in a forefather's dream. In dream
and sweat the fields have seasoning.

Let my words then begin in labor.
Let me sing a work song
and an earth song. Let the song of light
fall upon me as it may.
The end of this is not in sight.
And I come to the waning of the year
weary, the way long.

FROM THE CREST

What we leave behind to sleep
is ahead of us when we wake.
Cleared, the field must be
kept clear. There are more
clarities to make.
The farm is an infinite form.
Thinking of what may come,
I wake up in the night
and cannot go back to sleep.
The future swells in the dark,
too large a room for one
man to sleep well in.
I think of the work at hand.
Before spring comes again
there is another pasture
to clear and sow, for an end
I desire but cannot know.
Now in the silent keep
of stars and of my work
I lay me down to sleep.

2.

The deepest sleep holds us
to something immutable.
We have fallen
into place, and harmony
surrounds us. We are carried
in the world, in the company
of stars. But as dawn comes
I feel the waking of my hunger
for another day. I weave
round it again the kindling
tapestry of desire.

3.

My life's wave is at its crest.
The thought of work becomes
a friend of the thought of rest.
I see how little avail
one man is, and yet I would not
be a man sitting still,
no little song of desire
traveling the mind's dark woods.

I am trying to teach my mind
to bear the long, slow growth
of the fields, and to sing
of its passing while it waits.

The farm must be made a form,
endlessly bringing together
heaven and earth, light
and rain building, dissolving,
building back again
the shapes and actions of the ground.

If it is to be done,
not of the body, not of the will
the strength will come,
but of delight that moves
lovers in their loves,
that moves the sun and stars,
that stirs the leaf, and lifts
the hawk in flight.

From the crest of the wave
the grave is in sight,
the soul's last deep track
in the known. Past there
it gives up roof and fire,

board, bed, and word.
It returns to the wild,
where nothing is done by hand.

I am trying to teach
my mind to accept the finish
that all good work must have:
of hands touching me,
days and weathers passing
over me, the smooth of love,
the wearing of the earth.
At the final stroke
I will be a finished man.

4.

Little farm, motherland, made
by what has nearly been your ruin,
when I speak to you, I speak
to myself, for we are one
body. When I speak to you,
I speak to wife, daughter, son,
whom you have fleshed in your flesh.
And speaking to you, I speak
to all that brotherhood that rises
daily in your substance
and walks, burrows, flies, stands:
plants and beasts whose lives
loop like dolphins through your sod.

5.

Going into the city, coming
home again, I keep you
always in my mind.
Who knows me who does not
know you? The crowds of the streets
do not know that you

are passing among them with me.
They think I am simply a man,
made of a job and clothes
and education. They do not
see who is with me,
or know the resurrection
by which we have come
from the dead. In the city
we must be seemly and quiet
as becomes those who travel
among strangers. But do not
on that account believe
that I am ashamed
to acknowledge you, my friend.
We will write them a poem
to tell them of the great
membership, the mystic order,
to which both of us belong.

6.

When I think of death I see
that you are but a passing thought
poised upon the ground,
held in place
by vision, love, and work,
all as passing as a thought.

7.

Beginning and end
thread these fields like a net.
Nosing and shouldering,
the field mouse pats
his anxious routes through the grass,
the mole his cool ones
among the roots; the air
is tensely woven of bird flight,

fluttery at night with bats;
the mind of the honeybee
is the map of bloom.
Like a man, the farm is headed
for the woods. The wild
is already veined in it
everywhere, its thriving.
To love these things one did not
intend is to be a friend
to the beginning and the end.

8.

And when we speak together,
love, our words rise
like leaves, out of our fallen
words. What we have said
becomes an earth we live on
like two trees, whose sheddings
enrich each other, making
both the source of each.

When we love, the green
stalks and downturned bells
of lilies grow from our flesh.
Dreams and visions flower
from those beds our bodies are.

9.

The farm travels in snow,
a little world flying
through the Milky Way.
The flakes all fall
into place. But already
the mind begins to shift

its light, clearing space
to receive anew the old fate
of spring. In all the fields
and woods, old work calls
to new. The dead and living
prepare again to mate.

10.

Let the great song come
that sways the branches, that weaves
the nest of the vireo,
that the ground squirrel dreams
in his deep sleep, and wakes,
that the fish hear, that pipes
the minnows over
the shoals. In snow I wait
and sing of the braided
song I only partly hear.
Even in the rising year,
even in the spring,
the little can hope to sing
only in praise of the great.

A PART

(1980)

To my mother, who gave me books

STAY HOME

I will wait here in the fields
to see how well the rain
brings on the grass.
In the labor of the fields
longer than a man's life
I am at home. Don't come with me.
You stay home too.

I will be standing in the woods
where the old trees
move only with the wind
and then with gravity.
In the stillness of the trees
I am at home. Don't come with me.
You stay home too.

TO GARY SNYDER

After we saw the wild ducks
and walked away, drawing out
the quiet that had held us,
in wonder of them and of ourselves,
Den said, "I wish Mr. Snyder
had been here." And I said, "Yes."
But it cannot be often as it was
when we heard geese in the air
and ran out of the house to see them
wavering in long lines, high,
southward, out of sight.
By division we speak, out of wonder.

❀❁❀❁❀❁❀❁❀❁

FOR THE HOG KILLING

Let them stand still for the bullet, and stare the shooter in the
eye,
let them die while the sound of the shot is in the air, let them die
as they fall,
let the jugular blood spring hot to the knife, let its freshet be full,
let this day begin again the change of hogs into people, not the
other way around,
for today we celebrate again our lives' wedding with the world,
for by our hunger, by this provisioning, we renew the bond.

GOODS

It's the immemorial feelings
I like the best: hunger, thirst,
their satisfaction; work-weariness,
earned rest; the falling again
from loneliness to love;
the green growth the mind takes
from the pastures in March;
The gayety in the stride
of a good team of Belgian mares
that seems to shudder from me
through all my ancestry.

❋❀❋❀❋❀❋❀❋❀

THE ADZE

I came out to the barn lot
near nightfall, past supper time,
where he stood at work still
with the adze, that had to be
finely used or it would wound
the user—a lean old man
whose passion was to know
what a man could do in a day
and how a tool empowered the hand.
He paused to warn: stay back
from what innocence made dangerous.
I stayed back, and he went on
with what he had to do
while dark fell round him.

THE COLD PANE

Between the living world
and the world of death
is a clear, cold pane;
a man who looks too close
must fog it with his breath,
or hold his breath too long.

❁❁❁❁❁❁❁❁

FALLING ASLEEP

Raindrops on the tin roof.
What do they say?
We have all
Been here before.

A PURIFICATION

At start of spring I open a trench
in the ground. I put into it
the winter's accumulation of paper,
pages I do not want to read
again, useless words, fragments,
errors. And I put into it
the contents of the outhouse:
light of the sun, growth of the ground,
finished with one of their journeys.
To the sky, to the wind, then,
and to the faithful trees, I confess
my sins: that I have not been happy
enough, considering my good luck;
have listened to too much noise;
have been inattentive to wonders;
have lusted after praise.
And then upon the gathered refuse
of mind and body, I close the trench,
folding shut again the dark,
the deathless earth. Beneath that seal
the old escapes into the new.

A DANCE

The stepping-stones, once
in a row along the slope,
have drifted out of line,
pushed by frosts and rains.
Walking is no longer thoughtless
over them, but alert as dancing,
as tense and poised, to step
short, and long, and then
longer, right, and then left.
At the winter's end, I dance
the history of its weather.

❀❀❀❀❀❀❀

THE FEAR OF LOVE

I come to the fear of love
as I have often come,
to what must be desired
and to what must be done.

Only love can quiet the fear
of love, and only love can save
from diminishment the love
that we must lose to have.

We stand as in an open field,
blossom, leaf, and stem,
rooted and shaken in our day,
heads nodding in the wind.

SEVENTEEN YEARS

They are here again,
the locusts I baited my lines with
in the summer we married.
The light is filled
with the song the ground exhales
once in seventeen years.
And we are here with the wear
and the knowledge of those years,
understanding the song
of locusts no better than then,
knowing the future no more than they
who give themselves so long
to the dark. What can we say,
who grow older in love?
Marriage is not made
but in dark time, in the rhymes,
the returns of song,
that mark time's losses.
They open our eyes
to the dark, and we marry again.

5/29/74

TO WHAT LISTENS

I come to it again
and again, the thought of the wren
opening his song here
to no human ear—
no woman to look up,
no man to turn his head.
The farm will sink then
from all we have done and said.
Beauty will lie, fold
on fold, upon it. Foreseeing
it so, I cannot withhold
love. But from the height
and distance of foresight,
how well I like it
as it is! The river shining,
the bare trees on the bank,
the house set snug
as a stone in the hill's flank,
the pasture behind it green.
Its songs and loves throb
in my head till like the wren
I sing—to what listens—again.

WOODS

I part the out thrusting branches
and come in beneath
the blessèd and the blessing trees.
Though I am silent
there is singing around me.
Though I am dark
there is vision around me.
Though I am heavy
there is flight around me.

❁❦❁❦❁❦❁❦❁❦❁

THE LILIES

Hunting them, a man must sweat, bear
the whine of a mosquito in his ear,
grow thirsty, tired, despair perhaps
of ever finding them, walk a long way.
He must give himself over to chance,
for they live beyond prediction.
He must give himself over to patience,
for they live beyond will. He must be led
along the hill as by a prayer.
If he finds them anywhere, he will find
a few, paired on their stalks,
at ease in the air as souls in bliss.
I found them here at first without hunting,
by grace, as all beauties are first found.
I have hunted and not found them here.
Found, unfound, they breathe their light
into the mind, year after year.

FORTY YEARS

Life is your privilege, not your belonging.
It is the loss of it, now, that you will be singing.

❁❁❁❁❁❁❁❁❁

A MEETING

In a dream I meet
my dead friend. He has,
I know, gone long and far,
and yet he is the same
for the dead are changeless.
They grow no older.
It is I who have changed,
grown strange to what I was.
Yet I, the changed one,
ask: "How you been?"
He grins and looks at me.
"I been eating peaches
off some mighty fine trees."

ANOTHER DESCENT

Through the weeks of deep snow
we walked above the ground
on fallen sky, as though we did
not come of root and leaf, as though
we had only air and weather
for our difficult home.
                    But now
as March warms, and the rivulets
run like birdsong on the slopes,
and the branches of light sing in the hills,
slowly we return to earth.

BELOW

Above trees and rooftops
is the range of symbols:
banner, cross, and star;
air war, the mode of those
who live by symbols; the pure
abstraction of travel by air.
Here a spire holds up
an angel with trump and wings;
he's in *his* element.
Another lifts a hand
with forefinger pointing up
to admonish that all's not here.
All's not. But I aspire
downward. Flyers embrace
the air, and I'm a man
who needs something to hug.
All my dawns cross the horizon
and rise, from underfoot.
What I stand for
is what I stand on.

❁❧❁❧❁❧❁❧❁❧

THE STAR

Flying at night, above the clouds, all earthmarks spurned,
lost in Heaven, where peaceful entry must be earned,
I have no pleasure here, nothing to desire.
And then I see one light below there like a star.

THE HIDDEN SINGER

The gods are less
for their love of praise.
Above and below them all
is a spirit that needs
nothing but its own
wholeness,
its health and ours.
It has made all things
by dividing itself.
It will be whole again.
To its joy we come
together—the seer
and the seen, the eater
and the eaten, the lover
and the loved.
In our joining it knows
itself. It is with us then,
not as the gods
whose names crest
in unearthly fire,
but as a little bird
hidden in the leaves
who sings quietly
and waits
and sings.

THE NECESSITY OF FAITH

True harvests no mere intent may reap.
Finally we must lie down to sleep
And leave the world, all we desire
To darkness, malevolence, and fire.
Who wakes and stands his shadow's mark
Has passed by mercy through the dark.
We save the good, lovely, and bright
By will in part, in part delight,
But they live through the night by grace
That no intention can efface.

TO THE HOLY SPIRIT

O Thou, far off and here, whole and broken,
Who in necessity and in bounty wait,
Whose truth is light and dark, mute though spoken,
By Thy wide grace show me Thy narrow gate.

RIPENING

The longer we are together
the larger death grows around us.
How many we know by now
who are dead! We, who were young,
now count the cost of having been.
And yet as we know the dead
we grow familiar with the world.
We, who were young and loved each other
ignorantly, now come to know
each other in love, married
by what we have done, as much
as by what we intend. Our hair
turns white with our ripening
as though to fly away in some
coming wind, bearing the seed
of what we know. It was bitter to learn
that we come to death as we come
to love, bitter to face
the just and solving welcome
that death prepares. But that is bitter
only to the ignorant, who pray
it will not happen. Having come
the bitter way to better prayer, we have
the sweetness of ripening. How sweet
to know you by the signs of this world!

THE WAY OF PAIN

1.

For parents, the only way
is hard. We who give life
give pain. There is no help.
Yet we who give pain
give love, by pain we learn
the extremity of love.

2.

I read of Abraham's sacrifice
the Voice required of him,
so that he led to the altar
and the knife his only son.
The beloved life was spared
that time, but not the pain.
It was the pain that was required.

3.

I read of Christ crucified,
the only begotten Son
sacrificed to flesh and time
and all our woe. He died
and rose, but who does not tremble
for his pain, his loneliness,
and the darkness of the sixth hour?
Unless we grieve like Mary
at His grave, giving Him up
as lost, no Easter morning comes.

4.

And then I slept, and dreamed
the life of my only son
was required of me, and I
must bring him to the edge

of pain, not knowing why.
I woke, and yet that pain
was true. It brought his life
to the full in me. I bore him
suffering, with love like the sun,
too bright, unsparing, whole.

❁❁❁❁❁❁❁

WE WHO PRAYED AND WEPT

We who prayed and wept
for liberty from kings
and the yoke of liberty
accept the tyranny of things
we do not need.
In plentitude too free,
we have become adept
beneath the yoke of greed.

Those who will not learn
in plenty to keep their place
must learn it by their need
when they have had their way
and the fields spurn their seed.
We have failed Thy grace.
Lord, I flinch and pray,
send Thy necessity.

GRIEF

The morning comes. The old woman, a spot
of soot where she has touched her cheek, tears
on her face, builds a fire, sets water to boil,
puts the skillet on. The man in his middle years,
bent by the work he has done toward the work
he will do, weeps as he eats, bread in his mouth,
tears on his face. They shape the day for its passing
as if absent from it—for what needs care, caring,
feeding what must be fed. To keep them, there are only
the household's remembered ways, etched thin
and brittle by their tears. It is a sharp light
that lights the day now. It seems to shine,
beyond eyesight, also in another day
where the dead have risen and are walking
away, their backs forever turned. What
look is in their eyes? What do they say
as they walk into the fall and flow of light?
It seems that they must know where they are going.
And the living must go with them, not knowing,
a little way. And the dead go on, not turning,
knowing, but not saying. And the living
turn back to their day, their grieving and staying.

FALL

for Wallace Fowlie

The wild cherries ripen, black and fat,
Paradisal fruits that taste of no man's sweat.

Reach up, pull down the laden branch, and eat;
When you have learned their bitterness, they taste sweet.

❀❀❀❀❀❀❀❀

AN AUTUMN BURNING

for Kenneth Rexroth

In my line of paperwork
I have words to burn: leaves
of fallen information, wasted
words of my own. I know a light
that hastens on the dark
some work deserves—which God forgive
as we must hope. I start the blaze
and observe the fire's superlative
hunger for literature. It touches pages
like a connoisseur, turns them.
None can endure. After the passing
of that light, there is sunlight
on the ash, in the distance singing
of crickets and of birds. I turn,
unburdened, to life beyond words.

A WARNING TO MY READERS

Do not think me gentle
because I speak in praise
of gentleness, or elegant
because I honor the grace
that keeps this world. I am
a man crude as any,
gross of speech, intolerant,
stubborn, angry, full
of fits and furies. That I
may have spoken well
at times, is not natural.
A wonder is what it is.

CREATION MYTH

This is a story handed down.
It is about the old days when Bill
and Florence and a lot of their kin
lived in the little tin-roofed house
beside the woods, below the hill.
Mornings, they went up the hill
to work, Florence to the house,
the men and boys to the field.
Evenings, they all came home again.
There would be talk then and laughter
and taking of ease around the porch
while the summer night closed.
But one night, McKinley, Bill's younger brother,
stayed away late, and it was dark
when he started down the hill.
Not a star shone, not a window.
What he was going down into was
the dark, only his footsteps sounding
to prove he trod the ground. And Bill
who had got up to cool himself,
thinking and smoking, leaning on
the jamb of the open front door,
heard McKinley coming down,
and heard his steps beat faster
as he came, for McKinley felt the pasture's
darkness joined to all the rest
of darkness everywhere. It touched
the depths of woods and sky and grave.
In that huge dark, things that usually
stayed put might get around, as fish
in pond or slue get loose in flood.
Oh, things could be coming close
that never had come close before.
He missed the house and went on down

and crossed the draw and pounded on
where the pasture widened on the other side,
lost then for sure. Propped in the door,
Bill heard him circling, a dark star
in the dark, breathing hard, his feet
blind on the little reality
that was left. Amused, Bill smoked
his smoke, and listened. He knew where
McKinley was, though McKinley didn't.
Bill smiled in the darkness to himself,
and let McKinley run until his steps
approached something really to fear:
the quarry pool. Bill quit his pipe
then, opened the screen, and stepped out,
barefoot, on the warm boards. "McKinley!"
he said, and laid the field out clear
under McKinley's feet, and placed
the map of it in his head.

❂⟨❂⟨❂⟨❂⟨❂⟨❂

THE FIRST

The first man who whistled
thought he had a wren in his mouth.
He went around all day
with his lips puckered,
afraid to swallow.

WALKING ON THE RIVER ICE

A man could be a god
if the ice wouldn't melt
and he could stand the cold.

❀❀❀❀❀❀❀❀

THROWING AWAY THE MAIL

Nothing is simple,
not even simplification.
Thus, throwing away
the mail, I exchange
the complexity of duty
for the simplicity of guilt.

❀❀❀❀❀❀❀❀

EXCEPT

Now that you have gone
and I am alone and quiet,
my contentment would be
complete, if I did not wish
you were here so I could say,
"How good it is, Tanya,
to be alone and quiet."

FOR THE FUTURE

Planting trees early in spring,
we make a place for birds to sing
in time to come. How do we know?
They are singing here now.
There is no other guarantee
that singing will ever be.

❀❀❀❀❀❀❀❀❀

TRAVELING AT HOME

Even in a country you know by heart
it's hard to go the same way twice.
The life of the going changes.
The chances change and make a new way.
Any tree or stone or bird
can be the bud of a new direction. The
natural correction is to make intent
of accident. To get back before dark
is the art of going.

JULY, 1773

Seventeen seventy one
and two. In those years the fame
of the Long Hunters passed back
through the settlements, with news
of a rich and delightful country
to the west, on the waters of the Ohio.
My father and uncles held council
over their future prospects.
In the vigor of manhood and full
of enterprise, they longed to see
for themselves. They could not remain
confined in the sterile mountains
of Virginia, where only small parcels
of fertile land could be found
at any one place. As soldiers
of the Indian Wars, each had
from the governor a grant
of four hundred acres, which had only
to be located and surveyed.

                              And so,
having first planted their corn
about the tenth of May
in the year 1773, they set out
to visit this land of promise,
five of them, taking along
Sam Adams, a neighbor's son,
nineteen years of age.
They sought their future homes,
their fortunes, and the honor
of being among the first
in that western wilderness.

They reached the Great Kanahway,
then known as New River,
about the middle of May.
Having sent back their horses,
they selected suitable trees,
felled them, hollowed the trunks,
and so made two canoes
to carry them and their baggage:
rifles, ammunition, tomahawks,
butcher knives, blankets,
fishing tackle, and gigs.
And then, after their rough
overland passage on horseback,
how lightly and quietly they passed
over the surface of the water,
their prows breaking the reflections
of the trees in the early morning.

They entered the Ohio on
the first of June, the opening
of light on that wide water,
its stillness and solitudes.
Opposite the mouth of the Scioto
they saw an old French town
of nineteen or twenty houses,
hewed logs and clapboard roofs,
vacant and deserted, small
and silent among the great trees.

On June thirteenth, a Sunday,
they were met by the bearer of a letter
"to the gentleman settlers"
from Richard Butler, a white man
who had lived at Chilicothe
with the Shawanoes several years:

"They claim an absolute rite
to all that country that you
are about to settle. It does not
lie in the power of those
who sold it to give this land.
Show a friendly countenance
to your present neighbors, the Shawanoes.
It lies in your power to have
good neighbors or bad, as they
are a people very capable
of discerning between good treatment
and ill. They expect you
to be friendly with them,
and to endeavor to restrain
the hunters from destroying the game."
And this they took to show
the means by which an All-wise
Providence opened the way
for exploitation and settlement.

They camped on July fourth
at Big Bone Lick.
"It was a wonder to see
the large bones that lies there
which has been of several
large big creatures."
They used the short joints
of the backbones for stools,
and the ribs for tent poles
to stretch their blankets on.
Here they met a Delaware
about seventy years old.
Did he know anything
about these bones? He replied
that when he was a boy "they

were just so as you now see them."
And so they had come to a place
of mystery; they could not
enter except in awe.

At daylight on the morning
of July eighth, they reached
the mouth of the Kentucky River,
which they called the Lewvisa.
This was the foretold stream
that would carry them southward
into the heart of promise.
They set against its current,
reaching by nightfall the mouth
of a stream they called Eagle Creek
for the eagles they saw hovering
there, in the evening light.

And the next day went on
to the mouth of what is now
Drennon Creek, where the river
was nearly closed by a stone bar,
and there they left their boats.
They crossed a bottomland
through a forest of beech trees,
gray trunks in the shade
of gold-green foliage,
and after a mile came to
"a salt lick which was
a wonder to see—a mile
in length and one hundred yards
in breadth, & the roads that came
to that lick no man would believe
who did not see, & the woods
around that place were trod

for many miles, that there
was not as much food
as would feed one sheep."

They encountered there great numbers
of buffalo, elk, deer,
beaver, wolves, and bears.
The commotion of the herds was astonishing,
their tramplings and outcries,
the flies and the dust. There
where the salts of the ground flowed
to the light, the living blood
of that country gathered, throve
in its seasonal pulse—such
a gathering of beasts as these men
had never seen. Through the nights
they heard them, dreamed them,
seeming to comprehend them
more clearly in dream
than in eyesight, for that upwelling
and abounding, unbidden by any
man, was powerful, bright,
and brief for men like these,
as a holy vision. Waking,
they could not keep it. They did not.

Five days and six
nights they camped there,
examining the lick, killing
game, making several
surveys of land. The uplands
around the lick they found
"very good, mostly
oak timber; a great many
small creeks and branches;

scarce as much water
among them all as would
save a man's life
while he traveled across them."

One day, engaged in this work,
Uncle James and his neighbor's
son, Sam Adams, were passing
round the outskirts of the lick,
where had gathered a large herd
of the buffalo. The beasts
pressed together for the salt,
stomped, coughed, suckled
their calves, the dust rising
over their humps and horns,
their tails busy at flies.
They minded less than flies
the two men who moved
around them, thinking of other
lives, times to come.
And yet Sam Adams, boylike
perhaps, though he was nineteen
and a man in other ways,
would be diverted from his work
to gaze at the buffalo,
more numerous than all
his forefather's cattle, oblivious
abundance, there by no man's
will—godly, he might
have thought it, had he not
thought God a man.

         And why
he shot into the herd
is a question he did not answer,
anyhow until afterwards,

if at all—if he asked at all.
He saw an amplitude
so far beyond his need
he could not imagine it,
and could not let it be.
He shot.

　　　And the herd, unskilled
in fear of such a weapon
or such a creature, ran
in clumsy terror directly
toward the spot where the boy
and the man were standing.
Agile, the boy sprang
into a leaning mulberry.
Not so young, or active,
or so used to haste,
Uncle James took shelter
behind a young hickory
whose girth was barely larger
than his own.

　　　Then it seemed
the earth itself rose,
gathered, fled past them.
The great fall of hooves shook
ground and tree. Leaves
trembled in the one sound.
Dust hid everything
from everything. Bodies
beat against each other
in heavy flight. Black horns
sheared bark from the hickory
that protected Uncle James.

It fled. The hectic pulse
died in the ground. The dust
thinned. Day returned,
as it seemed, after nightmare.
And there was Sam Adams
looking out of his tree
at Uncle James, who looked
back, his hat now tilted.
"My good boy, you must not
venture that again."

And they walked southeast from there
two days, some thirty miles,
left a tomahawk and fish gig
at a fine spring, and marked
a gum sapling at that place.

*(This poem makes extensive borrowings
from various accounts of the McAfee
brothers' 1773 expedition into Kentucky.)*

THE SLIP

for Donald Davie

The river takes the land, and leaves nothing.
Where the great slip gave way in the bank
and an acre disappeared, all human plans
dissolve. An aweful clarification occurs
where a place was. Its memory breaks
from what is known now, begins to drift.
Where cattle grazed and trees stood, emptiness
widens the air for birdflight, wind, and rain.
As before the beginning, nothing is there.
Human wrong is in the cause, human
ruin in the effect—but no matter;
all will be lost, no matter the reason.
Nothing, having arrived, will stay.
The earth, even, is like a flower, so soon
passeth it away. And yet this nothing
is the seed of all—the clear eye
of Heaven, where all the worlds appear.
Where the imperfect has departed, the perfect
begins its struggle to return. The good gift
begins again its descent. The maker moves
in the unmade, stirring the water until
it clouds, dark beneath the surface,
stirring and darkening the soul until pain
perceives new possibility. There is nothing
to do but learn and wait, return to work
on what remains. Seed will sprout in the scar.
Though death is in the healing, it will heal.

HORSES

When I was a boy here,
traveling the fields for pleasure,
the farms were worked with teams.
As late as then a teamster
was thought an accomplished man,
his art an essential discipline.
A boy learned it by delight
as he learned to use
his body, following the example
of men. The reins of a team
were put into my hands
when I thought the work was play.
And in the corrective gaze
of men now dead I learned
to flesh my will in power
great enough to kill me
should I let it turn.
I learned the other tongue
by which men spoke to beasts
—all its terms and tones.
And by the time I learned,
new ways had changed the time.
The tractors came. The horses
stood in the fields, keepsakes,
grew old, and died. Or were sold
as dogmeat. Our minds received
the revolution of engines, our will
stretched toward the numb endurance
of metal. And that old speech
by which we magnified
our flesh in other flesh
fell dead in our mouths.
The songs of the world died
in our ears as we went within

the uproar of the long syllable
of the motors. Our intent entered
the world as combustion.
Like our travels, our workdays
burned upon the world,
lifting its inwards up
in fire. Veiled in that power
our minds gave up the endless
cycle of growth and decay
and took the unreturning way,
the breathless distance of iron.

But that work, empowered by burning
the world's body, showed us
finally the world's limits
and our own. We had then
the life of a candle, no longer
the ever-returning song
among the grassblades and the leaves.

Did I never forget?
Or did I, after years,
remember? To hear that song
again, though brokenly
in the distances of memory,
is coming home. I came to
a farm, some of it unreachable
by machines, as some of the world
will always be. And so
I came to a team, a pair
of mares—sorrels, with white
tails and manes, beautiful!—
to keep my sloping fields.
Going behind them, the reins
tight over their backs as they stepped
their long strides, revived

again on my tongue the cries
of dead men in the living
fields. Now every move
answers what is still.
This work of love rhymes
living and dead. A dance
is what this plodding is,
a song, whatever is said.

THE WHEEL

(1982)

It needs a more refined perception to recognize throughout this stupendous wealth of varying shapes and forms the principle of stability. Yet this principle dominates. It dominates by means of an ever-recurring cycle . . . repeating itself silently and ceaselessly. . . . This cycle is constituted of the successive and repeated processes of birth, growth, maturity, death, and decay.

An eastern religion calls this cycle the Wheel of Life and no better name could be given to it. The revolutions of this Wheel never falter and are perfect. Death supersedes life and life rises again from what is dead and decayed.

Sir Albert Howard,
The Soil and Health: A Study of Organic Agriculture

I

OWEN FLOOD / JANUARY 13, 1920–MARCH 27,1974

REQUIEM

1.

We will see no more
the mown grass fallen behind him
on the still ridges before night,
or hear him laughing in the crop rows,
or know the order of his delight.

Though the green fields are my delight,
elegy is my fate. I have come to be
survivor of many and of much
that I love, that I won't live to see
come again into this world.

Things that mattered to me once
won't matter any more,
for I have left the safe shore
where magnificence of art
could suffice my heart.

2.

In the day of his work
when the grace of the world
was upon him, he made his way,
not turning back or looking aside,
light in his stride.

Now may the grace of death
be upon him, his spirit blessed
in deep song of the world
and the stars turning, the seasons
returning, and long rest.

ELEGY

To be at home on its native ground
the mind must go down below its horizon,
descend below the lightfall
on ridge and steep and valley floor
to receive the lives of the dead. It must wake
in their sleep, who wake in its dreams.

"Who is here?" On the rock road between
creek and woods in the fall of the year,
I stood and listened. I heard the cries
of little birds high in the wind.
And then the beat of old footsteps
came around me, and my sight was changed.

I passed through the lens of darkness
as through a furrow, and the dead
gathered to meet me. They knew me,
but looked in wonder at the lines in my face,
the white hairs sprinkled on my head.

I saw a tall old man leaning
upon a cane, his open hand
raised in some fierce commendation,
knowledge of long labor in his eyes;
another, a gentler countenance,
smiling beneath a brim of sweaty felt
in welcome to me as before.

I saw an old woman, a saver
of little things, whose lonely grief
was the first I knew; and one bent
with age and pain, whose busy hands
worked out a selflessness of love.

Those were my teachers. And there were more,
beloved of face and name, who once bore
the substance of our common ground.
Their eyes, having grieved all grief, were clear.

2.

I saw one standing aside, alone,
weariness in his shoulders, his eyes
bewildered yet with the newness
of his death. In my sorrow I felt,
as many times before, gladness
at the sight of him. "Owen," I said.

He turned—lifted, tilted his hand.
I handed him a clod of earth
picked up in a certain well-known field.
He kneaded it in his palm and spoke:
"Wendell, this is not a place
for you and me." And then he grinned;
we recognized his stubbornness—
it was his principle to doubt
all ease of satisfaction.

"The crops are in the barn," I said,
"the morning frost has come to the fields,
and I have turned back to accept,
if I can, what none of us could prevent."

He stood, remembering, weighing the cost
of the division we had come to,
his fingers resting on the earth
he held cupped lightly in his palm.
It seemed to me then that he cast off
his own confusion, and assumed
for one last time, in one last kindness,
the duty of the older man.

He nodded his head. "The desire I had
in early morning and in spring,
I never wore it out. I had
the desire, if I had had the strength.
But listen—what we prepared
to have, we have."

He raised his eyes.
"Look," he said.

3.

We stood on a height,
woods above us, and below
on the half-mowed slope we saw ourselves
as we once were: a young man mowing,
a boy grubbing with an axe.

It was an old abandoned field,
long overgrown with thorns and briars.
We made it new in the heat haze
of that midsummer: he, proud
of the ground intelligence clarified,
and I, proud in his praise.

"I wish," I said, "that we could be
back in that good time again."

"We are back there again, today
and always. Where else would we be?"
He smiled, looked at me, and I knew
it was my mind he led me through.
He spoke of some infinitude
of thought.

He led me to another
slope beside another woods,
this lighted only by stars. Older

now, the man and the boy lay
on their backs in deep grass, quietly
talking. In the distance moved
the outcry of one deep-voiced hound.

Other voices joined that voice:
another place, a later time,
a hunter's fire among the trees,
faces turned to the blaze, laughter
and then silence, while in the dark
around us lay long breaths of sleep.

4.

And then, one by one, he moved me
through all the fields of our lives,
preparations, plantings, harvests,
crews joking at the row ends,
the water jug passing like a kiss.

He spoke of our history passing through us,
the way our families' generations
overlap, the great teaching
coming down by deed of companionship:
characters of fields and times and men,
qualities of devotion and of work—
endless fascinations, passions
old as mind, new as light.

All our years around us, near us,
I saw him furious and narrow,
like most men, and saw the virtue
that made him unlike most.
It was his passion to be true
to the condition of the Fall—
to live by the sweat of his face, to eat
his bread, assured that cost was paid.

5.

We came then to his time of pain,
when the early morning light showed,
as always, the sweet world, and all
an able, well-intentioned man
might do by dark, and his strength failed
before the light. His body had begun
too soon its earthward journey,
filling with gravity, and yet his mind
kept its old way.

       Again, in the sun
of his last harvest, I heard him say:
"Do you want to take this row,
and let me get out of your way?"
I saw the world ahead of him then
for the first time, and I saw it
as he already had seen it,
himself gone from it. It was a sight
I could not see and not weep.
He reached and would have touched me
with his hand, though he could not.

6.

Finally, he brought me to a hill
overlooking the fields that once
belonged to him, that he once
belonged to. "Look," he said again.
I knew he wanted me to see
the years of care that place wore,
for his story lay upon it, a bloom,
a blessing.

       The time and place so near,
we almost *were* the men we watched.
Summer's end sang in the light.

We spoke of death and obligation,
the brevity of things and men.
Words never moved so heavily
between us, or cost us more. We hushed.
And then that man who bore his death
in him, and knew it, quietly said:
"Well. It's a fascinating world,
after all."

His life so powerfully
stood there in presence of his place
and work and time, I could not
realize except with grief
that only his spirit now was with me.

In the very hour he died, I told him,
before I knew his death, the thought
of years to come had moved me
like a call. I thought of healing,
health, friendship going on,
the generations gathering, our good times
reaching one best time of all.

7.

My mind was overborne with questions
I could not speak. It seemed to me
we had returned now to the dark
valley where our journey began.
But a brightening intelligence
was on his face. Insight moved him
as he once was moved by daylight.

The best teachers teach more
than they know. By their deaths
they teach most. They lead us beyond
what we know, and what they knew.

Thus my teacher, my old friend,
stood smiling now before me, wholly
moved by what had moved him partly
in the world.

          Again the host of the dead
encircled us, as in a dance.
And I was aware now of the unborn
moving among them. As they turned
I could see their bodies come to light
and fade again in the dark throng.
They moved as to a distant or a hovering
song I strained for, but could not hear.

"Our way is endless," my teacher said.
"The Creator is divided in Creation
for the joys of recognition. We knew
that Spirit in each other once;
it brings us here. By its divisions
and returns, the world lives.
Both mind and earth are made
of what its light gives and uses up.
So joy contains, survives its cost.
The dead abide, as grief knows.
We are what we have lost."

There is a song in the Creation;
it has always been the gift
of every gifted voice, though none
ever sang it. As he spoke
I heard that song. In its changes and returns
his life was passing into life.
That moment, earth and song and mind,
the living and the dead, were one.

8.

At last, completed in his rest,
as one who has worked and bathed, fed
and loved and slept, he let fall
the beloved earth that I had brought him.
He raised his hand, turned me to my way.
And I, inheritor of what I mourned,
went back toward the light of day.

RISING

for Kevin Flood

1.

Having danced until nearly
time to get up, I went on
in the harvest, half lame
with weariness. And he
took no notice, and made
no mention of my distress.
He went ahead, assuming
that I would follow. I followed,
dizzy, half blind, bitter
with sweat in the hot light.
He never turned his head,
a man well known by his back
in those fields in those days.
He led me through long rows
of misery, moving like a dancer
ahead of me, so elated
he was, and able, filled
with desire for the ground's growth.
We came finally to the high
still heat of four o'clock,
a long time before sleep.
And then he stood by me
and looked at me as I worked,
just looked, so that my own head
uttered his judgment, even
his laughter. He only said:
"That social life don't get
down the row, does it, boy?"

2.

I worked by will then, he
by desire. What was ordeal
for me, for him was order
and grace, ideal and real.

That was my awkward boyhood,
the time of his mastery.
He troubled me to become
what I had not thought to be.

3.

The boy must learn the man
whose life does not travel
along any road, toward
any other place,
but is a journey back and forth
in rows, and in the rounds
of years. His journey's end
is no place of ease, but the farm
itself, the place day labor
starts from, journeys in,
returns to: the fields
whose past and potency are one.

4.

And that is our story,
not of time, but the forever
returning events of light,
ancient knowledge seeking
its new minds. The man at dawn
in spring of the year,
going to the fields,
visionary of seed and desire,
is timeless as a star.

5.

Any man's death could end the story:
his mourners, having accompanied him
to the grave through all he knew,
turn back, leaving him complete.

But this is not the story of a life.
It is the story of lives, knit together,
overlapping in succession, rising
again from grave after grave.

For those who depart from it, bearing it
in their minds, the grave is a beginning.
It has weighted the earth with sudden
new gravity, the enrichment of pain.

There is a grave, too, in each
survivor. By it, the dead one lives.
He enters us, a broken blade,
sharp, clear as a lens or a mirror.

And he comes into us helpless, tender
as the newborn enter the world. Great
is the burden of our care. We must be true
to ourselves. How else will he know us?

Like a wound, grief receives him.
Like graves, we heal over, and yet keep
as part of ourselves the severe gift.
By grief, more inward than darkness,

the dead become the intelligence of life.
Where the tree falls the forest rises.
There is nowhere to stand but in absence,
no life but in the fateful light.

6.

Ended, a story is history;
it is in time, with time
lost. But if a man's life
continue in another man,
then the flesh will rhyme
its part in immortal song.
By absence, he comes again.

There is a kinship of the fields
that gives to the living the breath
of the dead. The earth
opened in the spring, opens
in all springs. Nameless,
ancient, many-lived, we reach
through ages with the seed.

DESOLATION

A gracious Spirit sings as it comes
and goes. It moves forever
among things. Earth and flesh, passing
into each other, sing together.

Turned against that song, we go
where no singing is or light
or need coupled with its yes,
but spite, despair, fear, and loneliness.

Unless the solitary will forbear,
time enters the flesh to sever
passion from all care,
annul the lineage of consequence.

Unless the solitary will forbear,
the blade enters the ground
to tear the world's comfort
out, root and crown.

THE STRAIT

The valley holds its shadow.
My loves lie round me in the dark.
Through the woods on the hilltop
I see one distant light, a star
that seems to sway and flicker
as the trees move. I see the flight
of men crossing and crossing
the blank curve of heaven. I hear
the branches clashing in the wind.

2.

I have come to the end
of what I have supposed,
following my thread of song.
Who knows where it is going?

I am well acquainted now
among the dead. Only the past
knows me. In solitude
who will teach me?

3.

The world's one song is passing
in and out of deaths, as thrush notes
move in the shadows, nearer and nearer,
and then away, intent, in the hollows
of the woods. It does not attend
the dead, or what will die. It is light
though it goes in the dark. It goes
ahead, summoning. What hears follows.

4.

Sitting among the bluebells
in my sorrow, for lost time

and the never forgotten dead,
I saw a hummingbird stand
in air to drink from flowers.
It was a kiss he took and gave.
At his lightness and the ardor
of his throat, the song I live by
stirred my mind. I said:
"By sweetness alone it survives."

THE LAW THAT MARRIES ALL THINGS

1.

The cloud is free only
to go with the wind.

The rain is free
only in falling.

The water is free only
in its gathering together,

in its downward courses,
in its rising into air.

2.

In law is rest
if you love the law,
if you enter, singing, into it
as water in its descent.

3.

Or song is truest law,
and you must enter singing;
it has no other entrance.

It is the great chorus
of parts. The only outlawry
is in division.

4.

Whatever is singing
is found, awaiting the return
of whatever is lost.

5.

Meet us in the air
over the water,
sing the swallows.

Meet me, meet me,
the redbird sings,
here here here here.

SETTING OUT

for Gurney Norman

Even love must pass through loneliness,
the husbandman become again
the Long Hunter, and set out
not to the familiar woods of home
but to the forest of the night,
the true wilderness, where renewal
is found, the lay of the ground
a premonition of the unknown.
Blowing leaf and flying wren
lead him on. He can no longer be at home,
he cannot return, unless he begin
the circle that first will carry him away.

❁❁❁❁❁❁❁❁

SONG (1)

In ignorance of the source, our want
affirms abundance in these days.
Truth keeps us though we do not know it.
O Spirit, our desolation is your praise.

FROM THE DISTANCE

1.

We are others and the earth,
the living of the dead.
Remembering who we are,
we live in eternity;
any solitary act
is work of community.

2.

All times are one
if heart delight
in work, if hands
join the world right.

3.

The wheel of eternity is turning
in time, its rhymes, austere,
at long intervals returning,
sing in the mind, not in the ear.

4.

A man of faithful thought may feel
in light, among the beasts and fields,
the turning of the wheel.

5.

Fall of the year:
at evening a frail mist
rose, glowing in the rain.
The dead and unborn drew near
the fire. A song, not mine,
stuttered in the flame.

III

LETTER

1.

To search for what belongs where it is,
for what, scattered, might come together,
I leave you, my mold, my cup;
I flow from your bonds, a stream risen
over the hold of its stones.

2.

Turning always in my mind toward you,
your slopes, folds, gentle openings
on which I would rest my song
like an open hand, I know the trials of absence,
comely lives I must pass by, not to return,
beauties I will not know in satisfaction,
but in the sharp clarity of desire.

3.

In place with you, as I come and go
I pass the thread of my song again
and again through the web of my life
and the lives of the dead before me,
the old resounding in the new.
Now in the long curve of a journey
I spin a single strand, carried away
by what must bring me home.

RETURNING

I was walking in a dark valley
and above me the tops of the hills
had caught the morning light.
I heard the light singing as it went
among the grassblades and the leaves.
I waded upward through the shadow
until my head emerged,
my shoulders were mantled with the light,
and my whole body came up
out of the darkness, and stood
on the new shore of the day.
Where I had come was home,
for my own house stood white
where the dark river wore the earth.
The sheen of bounty was on the grass,
and the spring of the year had come.

TO TANYA AT CHRISTMAS

Forgive me, my delight,
that grief and loneliness
have kept me. Though I come
to you in darkness, you are
companion of the light
that rises on all I know.

In the long night of the year
and of the spirit, God's birth
is met with simple noise.
Deaf and blind in division,
I reach, and do not find.
You show the gentler way:
We come to good by love;
our words must be made flesh.

And flesh must be made word
at last, our lives rise
in speech to our children's tongues.
They will tell how we once stood
together here, two trees
whose lives in annual sheddings
made their way into this ground,
whose bodies turned to earth
and song. The song will tell
how old love sweetens the fields.

SONG (2)

My gentle hill, I rest
beside you in the dark
in a place warmed by my body,
where by ardor, grace, work,
and loss, I belong.

IV

THE RIVER BRIDGED AND FORGOT

Who can impair thee, mighty King

Bridged and forgot, the river
in unwearying descent
carries down the soil
of ravaged uplands, waste
and acid from the strip mines,
poisons of our false
prosperity. What mind
regains of clarity
mourns, the current a slow
cortege of everything
that we have given up,
the materials of Creation
wrecked, the strewed substance
of our trust and dignity.

But on still afternoons
of summer, the water's face
recovers clouds, the shapes
of leaves. Maple, willow,
sycamore stand light
and easy in their weight,
their branching forms formed
on the water, and yellow
warbler, swallow, oriole
stroke their deft flight
through the river's serene reflection
of the sky, as though, corrupted,
it shows the incorrupt.
Is this memory or promise?

And what is grief beside it?
What is anger beside it?
It is unfinished. It will not
be finished. And a man's life
will be, although his work
will not, nor his desire
for clarity. Beside
this dark passage of water
I make my work, lifework
of many lives that has
no end, for it takes circles
of years, of birth and death
for pattern, eternal form
visible in mystery.
It takes for pattern the heavenly
and earthly song of which
it is a part, which holds it
from despair: the joined voices
of all things, all muteness
vocal in their harmony.
For that, though none can hear
or sing it all, though I
must by nature fail,
my work has turned away
the priced infinity
of mechanical desire.

This work that many loves
inspire teaches the mind
resemblance to the earth
in seasonal fashioning,
departures and returns
of song. The hands strive
against their gravity
for envisioned lights and forms,
fallings of harmony;

they strive, fail at their season's
end. The seasonless river
lays hand and handiwork
upon the world, obedient
to a greater Mind, whole
past holding or beholding,
in whose flexing signature
all the dooms assemble
and become the lives of things.

THE GIFT OF GRAVITY

All that passes descends,
and ascends again unseen
into the light: the river
coming down from the sky
to hills, from hills to sea,
and carving as it moves,
to rise invisible,
gathered to light, to return
again. "The river's injury
is its shape." I've learned no more.
We are what we are given
and what is taken away;
blessed be the name
of the giver and taker.
For everything that comes
is a gift, the meaning always
carried out of sight
to renew our whereabouts,
always a starting place.
And every gift is perfect
in its beginning, for it
is "from above, and cometh down
from the Father of lights."
Gravity is grace.
All that has come to us
has come as the river comes,
given in passing away.
And if our wickedness
destroys the watershed,
dissolves the beautiful field,
then I must grieve and learn
that I possess by loss
the earth I live upon
and stand in and am. The dark

and then the light will have it.
I am newborn of pain
to love the new-shaped shore
where young cottonwoods
take hold and thrive in the wound,
kingfishers already nesting
in a hole in the sheared bank.
"What is left is what is" —
have learned no more. The shore
turns green under the songs
of the fires of the world's end,
and what is there to do?
Imagine what exists
so that it may shine
in thought light and day light,
lifted up in the mind.
The dark returns to light
in the kingfisher's blue and white
richly laid together.
He falls into flight
from the broken ground,
with strident outcry gathers
air under his wings.
In work of love, the body
forgets its weight. And once
again with love and singing
in my mind, I come to what
must come to me, carried
as a dancer by a song.
This grace is gravity.

V

SONG (3)

I stood and heard the steps of the city
and dreamed a lighter stepping than I heard,
the tread of my people dancing in a ring.
I knew that circle broken, the steps awry,
stone and iron humming in the air.

But I thought even there, among the straying
steps, of the dance that circles life around,
its shadows moving on the ground, in rhyme
of flesh with flesh, time with time, our bliss,
the earthly song that heavenly is.

THE WHEEL

for Robert Penn Warren

At the first strokes of the fiddle bow
the dancers rise from their seats.
The dance begins to shape itself
in the crowd, as couples join,
and couples join couples, their movement
together lightening their feet.
They move in the ancient circle
of the dance. The dance and the song
call each other into being. Soon
they are one—rapt in a single
rapture, so that even the night
has its clarity, and time
is the wheel that brings it round.
In this rapture the dead return.
Sorrow is gone from them.
They are light. They step
into the steps of the living
and turn with them in the dance
in the sweet enclosure
of the song, and timeless
is the wheel that brings it round.

THE DANCE

I would have each couple turn,
join and unjoin, be lost
in the greater turning
of other couples, woven
in the circle of a dance,
the song of long time flowing

over them, so they may return,
turn again in to themselves
out of desire greater than their own,
belonging to all, to each,
to the dance, and to the song
that moves them through the night.

What is fidelity? To what
does it hold? The point
of departure, or the turning road
that is departure and absence
and the way home? What we are
and what we were once

are far estranged. For those
who would not change, time
is infidelity. But we are married
until death, and are betrothed
to change. By silence, so,
I learn my song. I earn

my sunny fields by absence, once
and to come. And I love you
as I love the dance that brings you
out of the multitude
in which you come and go.
Love changes, and in change is true.

PASSING THE STRAIT

1.

Forsaking all others, we
are true to all. What we love
here, we would not desecrate
anywhere. Seed or song, work
or sleep, no matter the need,
what we let fall, we keep.

2.

The dance passes beyond us,
our loves loving their loves,
and returns, having passed through
the breaths and sleeps of the world,
the woven circuits of desire,
which leaving here arrive here.
Love moves in a bright sphere.

3.

Past the strait of kept faith
the flesh rises, is joined
to light. Risen from distraction
and weariness, we come
into the turning and changing
circle of all lovers. On this height
our labor changes into flight.

OUR CHILDREN, COMING OF AGE

In the great circle, dancing in
and out of time, you move now
toward your partners, answering
the music suddenly audible to you
that only carried you before
and will carry you again.
When you meet the destined ones
now dancing toward you,
we will be in line behind you,
out of your awareness for the time,
we whom you know, others we remember
whom you do not remember, others
forgotten by us all.
When you meet, and hold love
in your arms, regardless of all,
the unknown will dance away from you
toward the horizon of light.
Our names will flutter
on these hills like little fires.

SONG (4)

for Guy Davenport

Within the circles of our lives
we dance the circles of the years,
the circles of the seasons
within the circles of the years,
the cycles of the moon
within the circles of the seasons,
the circles of our reasons
within the cycles of the moon.

Again, again we come and go
changed, changing. Hands
join, unjoin in love and fear,
grief and joy. The circles turn,
each giving into each, into all.
Only music keeps us here,

each by all the others held.
In the hold of hands and eyes
we turn in pairs, that joining
joining each to all again.

And then we turn aside, alone,
out of the sunlight gone

into the darker circles of return.

VI

IN RAIN

1.

I go in under foliage
light with rain-light
in the hill's cleft,
and climb, my steps
silent as flight
on the wet leaves.
Where I go, stones
are wearing away
under the sky's flow.

2.

The path I follow
I can hardly see
it is so faintly trod
and overgrown.
At times, looking,
I fail to find it
among dark trunks, leaves
living and dead. And then
I am alone, the woods
shapeless around me.
I look away, my gaze
at rest among leaves,
and then I see the path
again, a dark way going on
through the light.

3.

In a mist of light
falling with the rain
I walk this ground
of which dead men
and women I have loved
are part, as they
are part of me. In earth,
in blood, in mind,
the dead and living
into each other pass,
as the living pass
in and out of loves
as stepping to a song.
The way I go is
marriage to this place,
grace beyond chance,
love's braided dance
covering the world.

4.

Marriages to marriages
are joined, husband and wife
are plighted to all
husbands and wives,
any life has all lives
for its delight.
Let the rain come,
the sun, and then the dark,
for I will rest
in any easy bed tonight.

ENTRIES

(1994)

PART ONE
Some Differences

In Memory: Harlan and Anna Hubbard

———

FOR THE EXPLAINERS

Spell the spiel of cause and effect,
Ride the long rail of fact after fact;
What curled the plume in the drake's tail
And put the white ring around his neck?

A MARRIAGE SONG

In January cold, the year's short light,
We make new marriage here;
The day is clear, the ground is bridal white,
Songless the brittled air
As we come through the snow to praise
Our Mary in her day of days.

In time's short light, and less than light, we pray
That odds be thus made evens,
And earthly love in its uncertain way
Be reconciled with Heaven's.
Before the early dark, we praise
Our Mary in her day of days.

Now let her honest, honored bridegroom come,
All other choice foregone,
To make his vows and claim and take her home,
Their two lives made in one.
He comes now through the snow to praise
Our Mary in her day of days.

All preparation past, and rightly glad,
She makes her pledge for good
Against all possibility of bad,
Begins her womanhood,
And as she walks the snow, we praise
Our Mary in her day of days.

Now, as her parents, we must stand aside,
For what we owed we've paid her
In far from perfect truth and love — this bride
Is more than we have made her,
And so we come in snow to praise
Our Mary in her day of days.

January 10, 1981

VOICES LATE AT NIGHT

Until I have appeased the itch
To be a millionaire,
Spare us, O Lord, relent and spare;
Don't end the world till it has made me rich.

It ends in poverty.

O Lord, until I come to fame
I pray Thee, keep the peace;
Allay all strife, let rancor cease
Until my book may earn its due acclaim.

It ends in strife, unknown.

Since I have promised wealth to all,
Bless our economy;
Preserve our incivility
And greed until the votes are cast this fall.

Unknown, it ends in ruin.

Favor the world, Lord, with Thy love;
Spare us for what we're not.
I fear Thy wrath, and Hell is hot;
Don't blow Thy trumpet until I improve.

Worlds blaze; the trumpet sounds.

O Lord, despite our right and wrong,
Let Thy daylight come down
Again on woods and field and town,
To be our daily bread and daily song.

It lives in bread and song.

THE RECORD

My old friend tells us how the country changed:
where the grist mill was on Cane Run,
now gone; where the peach orchard was,
gone too; where the Springport Road was, gone
beneath returning trees; how the creek ran three weeks
after a good rain, long ago, no more;
how when these hillsides first were plowed, the soil
was black and deep, no stones, and that was long ago;
where the wild turkeys roosted in the old days;
"You'd have to know this country mighty well
before I could tell you where."

And my young friend says: "Have him speak this
into a recorder. It is precious. It should be saved."
I know the panic of that wish to save
the vital knowledge of the old times, handed down,
for it is rising off the earth, fraying away
in the wind and the coming day.
As the machines come and the people go
the old names rise, chattering, and depart.

But knowledge of my own going into old time
tells me no. Because it must be saved,
do not tell it to a machine to save it.
That old man speaking you have heard
since your boyhood, since his prime, his voice
speaking out of lives long dead, their minds
speaking in his own, by winter fires, in fields and woods,
in barns while rain beat on the roofs
and wind shook the girders. Stay and listen
until he dies or you die, for death
is in this, and grief is in it. Live here
as one who knows these things. Stay, if you live;
listen and answer. Listen to the next one

like him, if there is to be one. Be
the next one like him, if you must;
stay and wait. Tell your children. Tell them
to tell their children. As you depart
toward the coming light, turn back
and speak, as the creek steps downward
over the rocks, saying the same changing thing
in the same place as it goes.

When the record is made, the unchanging
word carried to a safe place
in a time not here, the assemblage
of minds dead and living, the loved lineage
dispersed, silent, turned away, the dead
dead at last, it will be too late.

A PARTING

From many hard workdays in the fields,
many passages through the woods,
many mornings on the river, lifting
hooked lines out of the dark,
from many nightfalls, many dawns,
on the ridgetops and the creek road,
as upright as a tree, as freely standing,
Arthur Rowanberry comes in his old age
into the care of doctors, into the prison
of technical mercy, disease
and hectic skill making their way
into his body, hungry invaders fighting
for claims in that dark homeland,
strangers touching him, calling his name,
and so he lies down at last
in a bare room far from home.
And we who know him come
from the places he knew us in, and stand
by his bed, and speak. He smiles
and greets us from another time.
We stand around him like a grove,
a moment's shelter, old neighborhood
remade in that alien place. But the time
we stand in is not his time.
He is off in the places of his life,
now only places in his mind,
doing what he did in them when they were
the world's places, and he the world's man:
cutting the winter wood, piling the brush,
fixing the fences, mending the roofs,
caring for the crops under the long sun,
loading up the wagon, heading home.

ONE OF US

Must another poor body, brought
to its rest at last, be made the occasion
of yet another sermon? Have we nothing
to say of the dead that is not
a dull mortal lesson to the living,
our praise of Heaven blunted
by this craven blaming of the earth?
We must go with the body to the dark
grave, and there at the edge turn back
together—it is all that we can do—remembering
her as she is now in our minds
forever: how she gathered the chicks
into her apron before the storm, and tossed
the turkey hen over the fence,
so that the little ones followed,
peeping, out of the tall grass, safe
from the lurking snake; how she was one
of us, here with us, who is now gone.

THIRTY MORE YEARS

When I was a young man,
grown up at last, how large
I seemed to myself! I was a tree,
tall already, and what I had not
yet reached, I would yet grow
to reach. Now, thirty more years
added on, I have reached much
I did not expect, in a direction
unexpected. I am growing downward,
smaller, one among the grasses.

❁❀❁❀❁❀❁❀❁

THE WILD ROSE

Sometimes hidden from me
in daily custom and in trust,
so that I live by you unaware
as by the beating of my heart,

suddenly you flare in my sight,
a wild rose blooming at the edge
of thicket, grace and light
where yesterday was only shade,

and once more I am blessed, choosing
again what I chose before.

THE BLUE ROBE

How joyful to be together, alone
as when we first were joined
in our little house by the river
long ago, except that now we know

each other, as we did not then;
and now instead of two stories fumbling
to meet, we belong to one story
that the two, joining, made. And now

we touch each other with the tenderness
of mortals, who know themselves:
how joyful to feel the heart quake

at the sight of a grandmother,
old friend in the morning light,
beautiful in her blue robe!

THE VENUS OF BOTTICELLI

I knew her when I saw her
in the vision of Botticelli, riding
shoreward out of the waves,
and afterward she was in my mind

as she had been before, but changed,
so that if I saw her here, near
nightfall, striding off the gleam
of the Kentucky River as it darkened

behind her, the willows touching
her with little touches laid
on breast and arm and thigh, I

would rise as after a thousand
years, as out of the dark grave,
alight, shaken, to remember her.

IN A MOTEL PARKING LOT,
THINKING OF DR. WILLIAMS

I

The poem is important, but
not more than the people
whose survival it serves,

one of the necessities, so they may
speak what is true, and have
the patience for beauty: the weighted

grainfield, the shady street,
the well-laid stone and the changing tree
whose branches spread above.

For want of songs and stories
they have dug away the soil,
paved over what is left,

set up their perfunctory walls
in tribute to no god,
for the love of no man or woman,

so that the good that was here
cannot be called back
except by long waiting, by great

sorrow remembered and to come,
by invoking the understones
of the world, and the vivid air.

II

The poem is important,
as the want of it
proves. It is the stewardship

of its own possibility,
the past remembering itself
in the presence of

the present, the power learned
and handed down to see
what is present

and what is not: the pavement
laid down and walked over
regardlessly—by exiles, here

only because they are passing.
Oh, remember the oaks that were
here, the leaves, purple and brown,

falling, the nuthatches walking
headfirst down the trunks,
crying *"onc! onc!"* in the brightness

as they are doing now
in the cemetery across the street
where the past and the dead

keep each other. To remember,
to hear and remember, is to stop
and walk on again

to a livelier, surer measure.
It is dangerous
to remember the past only

for its own sake, dangerous
to deliver a message
that you did not get.

TO MY MOTHER

I was your rebellious son,
do you remember? Sometimes
I wonder if you do remember,
so complete has your forgiveness been.

So complete has your forgiveness been
I wonder sometimes if it did not
precede my wrong, and I erred,
safe found, within your love,

prepared ahead of me, the way home,
or my bed at night, so that almost
I should forgive you, who perhaps
foresaw the worst that I might do,

and forgave before I could act,
causing me to smile now, looking back,
to see how paltry was my worst,
compared to your forgiveness of it

already given. And this, then,
is the vision of that Heaven of which
we have heard, where those who love
each other have forgiven each other,

where, for that, the leaves are green,
the light a music in the air,
and all is unentangled,
and all is undismayed.

PART TWO

ON A THEME OF CHAUCER

I never have denied
What faith and scripture tell,
That Heaven's host is glad,
Or that there's pain in Hell.

But what I haven't tried
I'll not put up for sale.
No man has ever died
And lived to tell the tale.

THE REASSURER

A people in the throes of national prosperity, who
      breathe poisoned air, drink poisoned water, eat
      poisoned food,
who take poisoned medicines to heal them of the poisons
      that they breathe, drink, and eat,
such a people crave the further poison of official
      reassurance. It is not logical,
but it is understandable, perhaps, that they adore
      their President who tells them that all is well,
      all is better than ever.
The President reassures the farmer and his wife who
      have exhausted their farm to pay for it, and have
      exhausted themselves to pay for it,
and have not paid for it, and have gone bankrupt for
      the sake of the free market, foreign trade, and the
      prosperity of corporations;
he consoles the Navahos, who have been exiled from their
      place of exile, because the poor land contained
      something required for the national prosperity,
      after all;
he consoles the young woman dying of cancer caused by a
      substance used in the normal course of national
      prosperity to make red apples redder;
he consoles the couple in the Kentucky coalfields, who
      sit watching TV in their mobile home on the mud of
      the floor of a mined-out stripmine;
from his smile they understand that the fortunate have
      a right to their fortunes, that the unfortunate have
      a right to their misfortunes, and that these are
      equal rights.
The President smiles with the disarming smile of a man
      who has seen God, and found Him a true American,
      not overbearingly smart.

The President reassures the Chairman of the Board of the
     Humane Health for Profit Corporation of America,
     who knows in his replaceable heart that health, if
     it came, would bring financial ruin;
he reassures the Chairman of the Board of the Victory
     and Honor for Profit Corporation of America, who
     has been wakened in the night by a dream of the
     calamity of peace.

❀❀❀❀❀❀❀❀❀❀

LET US PLEDGE

Let us pledge allegiance to the flag
and to the national sacrifice areas
for which it stands, garbage dumps
and empty holes, sold out for a higher
spire on the rich church, the safety
of voyagers in golf carts, the better mood
of the stock market. Let us feast
today, though tomorrow we starve. Let us
gorge upon the body of the Lord, consuming
the earth for our greater joy in Heaven,
that fair Vacationland. Let us wander forever
in the labyrinths of our self-esteem.
Let us evolve forever toward the higher
consciousness of the machine.
The spool of our engine-driven fate
unwinds, our history now outspeeding
thought, and the heart is a beatable tool.

THE VACATION

Once there was a man who filmed his vacation.
He went flying down the river in his boat
with his video camera to his eye, making
a moving picture of the moving river
upon which his sleek boat moved swiftly
toward the end of his vacation. He showed
his vacation to his camera, which pictured it,
preserving it forever: the river, the trees,
the sky, the light, the bow of his rushing boat
behind which he stood with his camera
preserving his vacation even as he was having it
so that after he had had it he would still
have it. It would be there. With a flick
of a switch, there it would be. But he
would not be in it. He would never be in it.

❀❀❀❀❀❀❀❀❀

A LOVER'S SONG

When I was young and lately wed
And every fissionable head
Of this super power or that
Prepared the ultimate combat,
Gambling against eternity
To earn a timely victory
And end all time to win a day,
"Tomorrow let it end," I'd pray,
"If it must end, but not tonight."
And they were wrong and I was right;
It's love that keeps the world alive
Beyond hate's genius to contrive.

ANGLO-SAXON PROTESTANT
HETEROSEXUAL MEN

Come, dear brothers,
let us cheerfully acknowledge
that we are the last hope of the world,
for we have no excuses,
nobody to blame but ourselves.
Who is going to sit at our feet
and listen while we bewail
our historical sufferings? Who
will ever believe that we also
have wept in the night
with repressed longing to become
our real selves? Who will
stand forth and proclaim
that we have virtues and talents
peculiar to our category? Nobody,
and that is good. For here we are
at last with our real selves
in the real world. Therefore,
let us quiet our hearts, my brothers,
and settle down for a change
to picking up after ourselves
and a few centuries of honest work.

AIR

This man, proud and young,
turns homeward in the dark
heaven, free of his burden
of death by fire, of life in fear
of death by fire, in the city
now burning far below.

This is a young man, proud;
he sways upon the tall stalk
of pride, alone, in control of the
explosion by which he lives, one
of the children we have taught
to be amused by horror.

This is a proud man, young
in the work of death. Ahead of him
wait those made rich by fire.
Behind him, another child
is burning; a divine man
is hanging from a tree.

THE MAD FARMER, FLYING THE
FLAG OF ROUGH BRANCH, SECEDES
FROM THE UNION

From the union of power and money,
from the union of power and secrecy,
from the union of government and science,
from the union of government and art,
from the union of science and money,
from the union of ambition and ignorance,
from the union of genius and war,
from the union of outer space and inner vacuity,
the Mad Farmer walks quietly away.

There is only one of him, but he goes.
He returns to the small country he calls home,
his own nation small enough to walk across.
He goes shadowy into the local woods,
and brightly into the local meadows and croplands.
He goes to the care of neighbors,
he goes into the care of neighbors.
He goes to the potluck supper, a dish
from each house for the hunger of every house.
He goes into the quiet of early mornings
of days when he is not going anywhere.

Calling his neighbors together into the sanctity
of their lives separate and together
in the one life of their commonwealth and home,
in their own nation small enough for a story
or song to travel across in an hour, he cries:

Come all ye conservatives and liberals
who want to conserve the good things and be free,
come away from the merchants of big answers,
whose hands are metalled with power;

from the union of anywhere and everywhere
by the purchase of everything from everybody at the lowest price
and the sale of anything to anybody at the highest price;
from the union of work and debt, work and despair;
from the wage-slavery of the helplessly well-employed.

From the union of self-gratification and self-annihilation,
secede into care for one another
and for the good gifts of Heaven and Earth.

Come into the life of the body, the one body
granted to you in all the history of time.
Come into the body's economy, its daily work,
and its replenishment at mealtimes and at night.
Come into the body's thanksgiving, when it knows
and acknowledges itself a living soul.
Come into the dance of community, joined
in a circle, hand in hand, the dance of the eternal
love of women and men for one another
and of neighbors and friends for one another.

Always disappearing, always returning,
calling his neighbors to return, to think again
of the care of flocks and herds, of gardens
and fields, of woodlots and forests and the uncut groves,
calling them separately and together, calling and calling,
he goes forever toward the long restful evening
and the croak of the night heron over the river at dark.

PART THREE

DUALITY

I

To love is to suffer—did I
know this when first
I asked you for your love?
I did not. And yet until
I knew, I could not know what
I asked, or gave. I gave
a suffering that I took: yours
and mine, mine when yours;
and yours I have feared most.

II

What can bring us past
this knowledge, so that you
will never wish our life
undone? For if ever you
wish it so, then I must wish
so too, and lovers yet unborn,
whom we are reaching toward
with love, will turn to this
page, and find it blank.

III

I have feared to be unknown
and to offend—I must speak,

then, against the dread
of speech. What if, hearing,
you have no reply, and mind's
despair annul the body's hope?
Life in time may justify
any conclusion, whenever
our will is to conclude.

IV

Look at me now. Now,
after all the years, look at me
who have no beauty apart
from what we two have made
and been. Look at me
with the look that anger
and pain have taught you,
the gaze in which nothing
is guarded, nothing withheld.

V

You look at me, you give
a light, which I bear and return,
and we are held, and all
our time is held, in this
touching look—this touch
that, pressed against the touch
returning in the dark,
is almost sight. We burn
and see by our own light.

VI

Eyes looking into eyes looking
into eyes, touches that see
in the dark, remember Paradise,
our true home. God's image
recalls us to Itself. We move
with motion not our own,

light upon light, day and
night, sway as two trees
in the same wind sway.

VII

Let us come to no conclusion,
but let our bodies burn
in time's timelessness. Heaven
and earth give us to this night
in which we tell each other of
a Kingdom yet to come, saying
its secret, its silent names.
We become fleshed words, one
another's uttered joy.

VIII

Joined in our mortal time,
we come to the resurrection
of words; they rise up
in our mouths, set free
of taints, errors, and bad luck.
In their new clarities
the leaf brightens, the air
clears, the syllables of water are
clear in the dark air as stars.

IX

We come, unsighted, in the dark,
to the great feast of lovers
where nothing is withheld.
That we are there we know
by touch, by inner sight.
They all are here, who by
their giving take, by taking
give, who by their living
love, and by loving live.

THE THREE

A woman wholly given in love is held
by a dying man and an immortal one.
The man dying knows himself departing
from her, leaving her in the arms
of the man who will live, cherishing her,
given to him as she is forever.

❀❁❀❁❀❁❀❁❀❁

TO HAYDEN CARRUTH

Dear Hayden, when I read your book I was aching
in head, back, heart, and mind, and aching
with your aches added to my own, and yet for joy
I read on without stopping, made eager
by your true mastery, wit, sorrow, and joy,
each made true by the others. My reading done,
I swear I am feeling better. Here in Port Royal
I take off my hat to you up there in Munnsville
in your great dignity of being necessary. I swear
it appears to me you're one of the rare fellows
who may finally amount to something. What shall
I say? I greet you at the beginning of a great career?
No. I greet you at the beginning, for we are
either beginning or we are dead. And let us have
no careers, lest one day we be found dead in them.
I greet you at the beginning that you have made
authentically in your art, again and again.

NOGUCHI FOUNTAIN

Sits level,
fills silently,
overflows,
makes music.

❀❀❀❀❀❀

SPRING

A shower like a little song
Overtook him going home,
Wet his shoulders, and went on.

❀❀❀❀❀❀

IMAGINATION

A young man's love is bitter love
For what he must forego,
For what he ignorantly would have,
Desires but does not know.

The years, the years will teach him joys
That are more bitter still;
What in his having he forgoes
He has imagined well.

FOR AN ABSENCE

When I cannot be with you
I will send my love (so much
is allowed to human lovers)
to watch over you in the dark—
a winged small presence
who never sleeps, however long
the night. Perhaps it cannot
protect or help, I do not know,
but it watches always, and so
you will sleep within my love
within the room within the dark.
And when, restless, you wake
and see the room palely lit
by that watching, you will think,
"It's only dawn," and go
quiet to sleep again.

✿❀✿❀✿❀✿❀✿

THE STORM

We lay in our bed as in a tomb
awakened by thunder to the dark
in which our house was one with night,
and then light came as if the black
roof of the world had cracked open,
as if the night of all time had broken,
and out our window we glimpsed the world
birthwet and shining, as even
the sun at noon had never made it shine.

PART FOUR

When thou wast young, thou girdest thyself, and walkedst
whither thou wouldest: but when thou shalt be old,
thou shalt stretch forth thy hands, and another shall
gird thee, and carry thee whither thou wouldest not

JOHN 21:18

———

IN EXTREMIS: *POEMS ABOUT MY FATHER*

I

I was at home alone. He came
to fight, as I had known he would.
The war in Vietnam was on;
I'd spoken out, opposing it—
and so, I thought, embarrassed him.

Not because he loved the war.
He feared for me, or for himself
in me. Fear angered him. He was
my enemy; his mind was made
up like a fist. He sat erect
on the chair's edge as on a horse,
would not take off his coat.
That was his way. My house was not
a house in which he would consent
to make himself at home that day.

The argument was hard and hot.
Tempered alike, we each knew where
the other's hide was tenderest.
We went past reason and past sense
by way of any eloquence
that hurt. He leaned. I saw the brown
spot in the blue of his right eye.

Forefinger hooking through the air,
he said I had been led astray,
beguiled, by he knew who, by God!

And was I then to be his boy
forever? Or his equal? Or
his foe? His equal and his foe?
By grace (I think it must have been
by grace) I told him what I knew:

"Do you know who has been, by God,
the truest teacher in my life
from the beginning until now?"

"*Who*, by God?"

       "*You*, by God!"

He wept and said, "By God, I'm proud."

II

He was, in his strength, the most feeling
and the most demanding man
I have ever known. I knew at first
only the difficulty of his demand,
but now I know the fear in it.
He has been afraid always of the loss
of precious things. We live in time
as in hard rain, and have no shelter,
half hopeless in anxiety for the young,
half hopeless in compassion for the old.
The generations fail and we forget
what we were, and are. The earth,
even, is flowing away. And where
is the stay against indifference?
I know his fear now by my own.
Precious things are being lost.

III

My grandfather, in the lost tongue
of his kind and time, called drawers
"draws." My father pronounced the word
that way himself from time to time
in commemoration. And now another
time had come. I diapered him
like a child and helped him go
with short slow steps to bed. Meaning
to invoke his old remembrance
to cheer him, I said, "Don't lose
your draws." "We miss him, don't we?"
he said. "Yes," I said. "Yes," he said.

IV

Sometimes we do not know what time he's in
Or if he is in time. The dead live in his mind.
They wait beyond his sight, made radiant by his long
Unchanging love, as by the mercy and the grace
Of God. At night I help him to lie down upon
That verge we reach by generation and by day.
He says that, though we sleep, we love eternally.

V

He dreamed there was a storm
And all was overturned.
In his great need he called
His mother and his father
To help him, and one he'd known
But did not know found him
On the dark stair, led him
Back to his bed. Next day,
The dream still near, he said,
In longing of this world
That in the next is joy,
"If I could have found Papa,
I'd have been so comforted."

VI

I imagine him as he must appear
to his father and mother now,
if from the world of the dead they see
him as he now is—an old man
sliding his feet along the floor
in little childish steps. I imagine
that they call him "child," and pity
him, and love him as they did,
for they are senior to him still,
having gone through the dark door,
and learned the hard things and the good
that only the dead can know.
And I imagine that they know also
the greater good, that we long for
but cannot know, that knows
of all our sorrow, and rejoices still.

VII

Sometimes in sleeping he forgets
That he is old and, waking up,
Intends to go out in the world
To work, just as he did before—
Only to find that his body now
No longer answers to his will,
And his mind too is changed but not
By him. And then he rages in
His grief, and will not be consoled.
He cannot be consoled by us,
More mortal in our fewer years,
Who have not reached the limit he
Has come to, when immortal love
In flesh, denying time, will look
At what is lost, and grief fulfill
The budget of desire. Sometimes,
At home, he longs to be at home.

VIII

And sometimes he fulfills
What must have been the worst
Of all his fears: to be
An old man, fierce and foul,
Outraged and unforgiving,
One man alone, mere fact
Beyond the reach of love.
For fear this is his fate,
And mine if it is his,
I struggle with him. Thus
We ardently debate
The truth of fantasy
Empowered by wrath—the facts
He says are lies, the lies
He says are facts—his
Eyes in their conviction hard
To meet, hard to avoid.
We go into a place
Of ruin, where light obscures,
The right place for us now
In our mad argument,
Exchanging foolish fire
In reasoned eloquence,
And winning no success.
We still are as we were,
And yet we do not fail,
For thus estranged we both
Oppose his loneliness.

IX

The dead come near him in his sleep
And, waking, he calls out to them
To help him in his helplessness.

And though they in their distance keep
Silent, and give no help to him.
And do not answer his distress,

I hear him calling in my sleep
Among the living in the dim
House, where he calls in loneliness.

I go to help him in the deep
Night, waked and walking in whose time?
I am the brother called in darkness.

X

We watch the TV show,
Smooth faces and smooth talk
Made for everywhere,
Thus alien everywhere.
In deference to old age
And time, we sit down for
What no one can stand up for.
I wish him out of it,
That man-made other world.
I wish undone his absence
In body and in thought
From open countryside,
Our local air and light.
To honor him aright
I call him back to mind,
Remember him again
When he was my age now,
And straighter-backed than I,
Still hungry for the world.
His mind was then an act
Accomplished soon as thought,
Though now his body serves

Unwillingly at best
His mind's unresting will.
I summon him away
From time and heaviness.
I see him as he was.

XI

The light is low and red upon the fields,
The mists are rising in the long hollow,
The shadows have stretched out, and he comes walking
In deep bluegrass that silences his steps.
Elated and upright, he walks beneath
The walnut trees around the spring. His work
Is done, the office shut and still, his chair
Empty. And now at his long shadow's foot,
He comes to salt the ewe flock, and to hear
The meadowlarks sing in the evening quiet.
He calls his sheep, who know his voice and come,
Crowding up to him as the light departs
And earth's great shadow gathers them in. White
In darkening air, their fleeces glow as he
Puts down the salt, a handful at a place,
Along the path. At last, the bucket empty,
He stands, watching the sheep, the deepening sky,
The few small stars already pointing out.

Now may he come to that good rest again.

XII

What did I learn from him?
He taught the difference
Between good work and sham,
Between nonsense and sense.

He taught me sentences,
Outspoken fact for fact,
In swift coherences
Discriminate and exact.

He served with mind and hand
What we were hoping for:
The small house on the land,
The shade tree by the door,

Garden, smokehouse, and cellar,
Granary, crib, and loft
Abounding, and no year
Lived at the next year's cost.

He kept in mind, alive,
The idea of the dead:
"A steer should graze and thrive
Wherever he lowers his head."

He said his father's saying.
We were standing on the hill
To watch the cattle grazing
As the gray evening fell.

"Look. See that this is good,
And then you won't forget."
I saw it as he said,
And I have not forgot.

EPITAPH

Having lived long in time,
he lives now in timelessness
without sorrow, made perfect
by our never finished love,
by our compassion and forgiveness,
and by his happiness in receiving
these gifts we give. Here in time
we are added to one another forever.

⊕⟨⊕⟨⊕⟨⊕⟨⊕⟨⊕

COME FORTH

I dreamed of my father when he was old.
We went to see some horses in a field;
they were sorrels, as red almost as blood,
the light gold on their shoulders and haunches.
Though they came to us, all a-tremble
with curiosity and snorty with caution,
they had never known bridle or harness.
My father walked among them, admiring,
for he was a knower of horses, and these were fine.

He leaned on a cane and dragged his feet
along the ground in hurried little steps
so that I called to him to take care, take care,
as the horses stamped and frolicked around him.
But while I warned, he seized the mane
of the nearest one. "It'll be all right,"
he said, and then from his broken stance
he leapt astride, and sat lithe and straight
and strong in the sun's unshadowed excellence.

GIVEN

(2005)

In Memory: Ross Feld

PART ONE
In a Country Once Forested

———

DUST

The dust motes float
and swerve in the sunbeam,
as lively as worlds,
and I remember my brother
when we were boys:
"We may be living on an atom
in somebody's wallpaper."

❀❦❀❦❀❦❀❦❀

IN A COUNTRY ONCE FORESTED

The young woodland remembers
the old, a dreamer dreaming

of an old holy book,
an old set of instructions,

and the soil under the grass
is dreaming of a young forest,

and under the pavement the soil
is dreaming of grass.

TO TANYA ON MY SIXTIETH BIRTHDAY

What wonder have you done to me?
In binding love you set me free.
These sixty years the wonder prove:
I bring you aged a young man's love.

❁⟨❁⟨❁⟨❁⟨❁⟨❁

THEY

I see you down there, white-haired
among the green leaves,
picking the ripe raspberries,
and I think, "Forty-two years!"
We are the you and I who were
they whom we remember.

❁⟨❁⟨❁⟨❁⟨❁⟨❁

CATHEDRAL

Stone
of the earth
made
of its own weight
light

DANTE

If you imagine
others are there,
you are there yourself.

❀❀❀❀❀❀❀❀❀

THE MILLENNIUM

What year
does the phoebe
think it is?

❀❀❀❀❀❀❀❀❀

JUNE WIND

Light and wind are running
over the headed grass
as though the hill had
melted and now flowed.

WHY

Why all the embarrassment
about being happy?
Sometimes I'm as happy
as a sleeping dog,
and for the same reasons,
and for others.

❀❀❀❀❀❀

THE REJECTED HUSBAND

After the storm and the new
stillness of the snow, he returns
to the graveyard, as though
he might lift the white coverlet,
slip in beside her as he used to do,
and again feel, beneath his hand,
her flesh quicken and turn warm.
But he is not her husband now.
To participate in resurrection, one
first must be dead. And he goes
back into the whitened world, alive.

THE INLET

In a dream I go
out into the sunlit street
and I see a boy walking
clear-eyed in the light.
I recognize him, he is
Bill Lippert, wearing the gray
uniform of the school
we attended many years ago.
And then I see that my brother
is with me in the dream,
dressed too in the old uniform.
Our friend looks as he did
when we first knew him,
and until I wake I believe
I will die of grief, for I know
that this boy grew into a man
who was a faithful friend
who died.
        Where I stood,
seeing and knowing, was time,
where we die of grief. And surely
the bright street of my dream,
in which we saw again
our old friend as a boy
clear-eyed in innocence of his death,
was some quickly-crossed
small inlet of eternity.

LISTEN!

How fine to have a radio
and beautiful music playing
while I sit at rest in the evening.
How fine to hear through the music
the cries of wild geese on the river.

IN ART ROWANBERRY'S BARN

In Art Rowanberry's barn, when Art's death
had become quietly a fact among
the other facts, Andy Catlett found
a jacket made of the top half
of a pair of coveralls after
the legs wore out, for Art
never wasted anything.
Andy found a careful box made
of woodscraps with a strap
for a handle; it contained
a handful of small nails
wrapped in a piece of newspaper,
several large nails, several
rusty bolts with nuts and washers,
some old harness buckles
and rings, rusty but usable,
several small metal boxes, empty,
and three hickory nuts
hollowed out by mice.
And all of these things Andy
put back where they had been,
for time and the world and other people
to dispense with as they might,
but not by him to be disprized.
This long putting away
of things maybe useful was not all
of Art's care-taking; he cared
for creatures also, every day
leaving his tracks in dust, mud,
or snow as he went about
looking after his stock, or gave
strength to lighten a neighbor's work.
Andy found a bridle made
of several lengths of baling twine

knotted to a rusty bit,
an old set of chain harness,
four horseshoes of different sizes,
and three hammerstones picked up
from the opened furrow on days
now as perfectly forgotten
as the days when they were lost.
He found a good farrier's knife,
an awl, a key to a lock
that would no longer open.

BURLEY COULTER'S SONG
FOR KATE HELEN BRANCH

The rugs were rolled back to the wall,
The band in place, the lamps all lit.
We talked and laughed a little bit
And then obeyed the caller's call—
Light-footed, happy, half entranced—
To balance, swing, and promenade.
Do you remember how we danced
And how the fiddler played?

About midnight we left the crowd
And wandered out to take a stroll.
We heard the treefrogs and the owl;
Nearby the creek was running loud.
The good dark held us as we chanced
The joy we two together made,
Remembering how we'd whirled and pranced
And how the fiddler played.

That night is many years ago
And gone, and still I see you clear,
Clear as the lamplight in your hair.
The old time comes around me now,
And I remember how you glanced
At me, and how we stepped and swayed.
I can't forget the way we danced,
The way the fiddler played.

HOW TO BE A POET

(to remind myself)

Make a place to sit down.
Sit down. Be quiet.
You must depend upon
affection, reading, knowledge,
skill—more of each
than you have—inspiration,
work, growing older, patience,
for patience joins time
to eternity. Any readers
who like your work,
doubt their judgment.

Breathe with unconditional breath
the unconditioned air.
Shun electric wire.
Communicate slowly. Live
a three-dimensioned life;
stay away from screens.
Stay away from anything
that obscures the place it is in.
There are no unsacred places;
there are only sacred places
and desecrated places.

Accept what comes from silence.
Make the best you can of it.
Of the little words that come
out of the silence, like prayers
prayed back to the one who prays,
make a poem that does not disturb
the silence from which it came.

WORDS

What is one to make of a life given
to putting things into words,
saying them, writing them down?
Is there a world beyond words?
There is. But don't start, don't
go on about the tree unqualified,
standing in light that shines
to time's end beyond its summoning
name. Don't praise the speechless
starlight, the unspeakable dawn.
Just stop.

2.

       Well, we *can* stop
for a while, if we try hard enough,
if we are lucky. We can sit still,
keep silent, let the phoebe, the sycamore,
the river, the stone call themselves
by whatever they call themselves, their own
sounds, their own silence, and thus
may know for a moment the nearness
of the world, its vastness,
its vast variousness, far and near,
which only silence knows. And then
we must call all things by name
out of the silence again to be with us,
or die of namelessness.

TO A WRITER OF REPUTATION

. . . the man must remain obscure.
CÉZANNE

Having begun in public anonymity,
you did not count on this
literary sublimation by which
some body becomes a "name" —
as if you have died and have become
a part of mere geography. Greet,
therefore, the roadsigns on the road.

Or perhaps you have become deaf and blind,
or merely inanimate, and may
be studied without embarrassment
by the disinterested, the dispassionate,
and the merely curious,
not fearing to be overheard.
Hello to the grass, then, and to the trees.

Or perhaps you are secretly
still alert and moving, no longer the one
they have named, but another,
named by yourself,
carrying away this morning's showers
for your private delectation.
Hello, river.

PART TWO
Further Words

———

SEVENTY YEARS

Well, anyhow, I am
not going to die young.

❁❁❁❁❁❁❁

A PASSING THOUGHT

I think therefore
I think I am.

THE LEADER

Head like a big
watermelon,
frequently thumped
and still not ripe.

❂❀❂❀❂❀❂❀❂

THE ONGOING HOLY WAR AGAINST EVIL

Stop the killing, or
I'll kill you, you
God-damned murderer!

SOME FURTHER WORDS

Let me be plain with you, dear reader.
I am an old-fashioned man. I like
the world of nature despite its mortal
dangers. I like the domestic world
of humans, so long as it pays its debts
to the natural world, and keeps its bounds.
I like the promise of Heaven. My purpose
is a language that can pay just thanks
and honor for those gifts, a tongue
set free from fashionable lies.

Neither this world nor any of its places
is an "environment." And a house
for sale is not a "home." Economics
is not "science," nor "information" knowledge.
A knave with a degree is a knave. A fool
in a public office is not a "leader."
A rich thief is a thief. And the ghost
of Arthur Moore, who taught me Chaucer,
returns in the night to say again:
"Let me tell you something, boy.
An intellectual whore is a whore."

The world is babbled to pieces after
the divorce of things from their names.
Ceaseless preparation for war
is not peace. Health is not procured
by sale of medication, or purity
by the addition of poison. Science
at the bidding of the corporations
is knowledge reduced to merchandise;
it is a whoredom of the mind,
and so is the art that calls this "progress."
So is the cowardice that calls it "inevitable."

I think the issues of "identity" mostly
are poppycock. We are what we have done,
which includes our promises, includes
our hopes, but promises first. I know
a "fetus" is a human child.
I loved my children from the time
they were conceived, having loved
their mother, who loved them
from the time they were conceived
and before. Who are we to say
the world did not begin in love?

I would like to die in love as I was born,
and as myself, of life impoverished, go
into the love all flesh begins
and ends in. I don't like machines,
which are neither mortal nor immortal,
though I am constrained to use them.
(Thus the age perfects its clench.)
Some day they will be gone, and that
will be a glad and a holy day.
I mean the dire machines that run
by burning the world's body and
its breath. When I see an airplane
fuming through the once-pure sky
or a vehicle of the outer space
with its little inner space
imitating a star at night, I say,
"Get *out* of there!" as I would speak
to a fox or a thief in the henhouse.

When I hear the stock market has fallen,
I say, "Long live gravity! Long live
stupidity, error, and greed in the palaces
of fantasy capitalism!" I think
an economy should be based on thrift,

on taking care of things, not on theft,
usury, seduction, waste, and ruin.

My purpose is a language that can make us whole,
though mortal, ignorant, and small.
The world is whole beyond human knowing.
The body's life is its own, untouched
by the little clockwork of explanation.
I approve of death, when it comes in time
to the old. I don't want to live
on mortal terms forever, or survive
an hour as a cooling stew of pieces
of other people. I don't believe that life
or knowledge can be given by machines.
The machine economy has set afire
the household of the human soul,
and all the creatures are burning in it.

"Intellectual property" names
the deed by which the mind is bought
and sold, the world enslaved. We
who do not own ourselves, being free,
own by theft what belongs to God,
to the living world, and equally
to us all. Or how can we own a part
of what we only can possess entirely?
"The laborer is worthy of his hire,"
but he cannot own what he knows,
which must be freely told, or labor
dies with the laborer. The farmer
is worthy of the harvest made
in time, but he must leave the light
by which he planted, grew, and reaped,
the seed immortal in mortality,
freely to the time to come. The land
too he keeps by giving it up,

as the thinker receives and gives a thought,
as the singer sings in the common air.

I don't believe that "scientific genius"
in its naïve assertions of power
is equal either to nature or
to human culture. Its thoughtless invasions
of the nuclei of atoms and cells
and this world's every habitation
have not brought us to the light
but sent us wandering farther through
the dark. Nor do I believe
"artistic genius" is the possession
of any artist. No one has made
the art by which one makes the works
of art. Each one who speaks speaks
as a convocation. We live as councils
of ghosts. It is not "human genius"
that makes us human, but an old love,
an old intelligence of the heart
we gather to us from the world,
from the creatures, from the angels
of inspiration, from the dead—
an intelligence merely nonexistent
to those who do not have it, but
to those who have it more dear than life.

And just as tenderly to be known
are the affections that make a woman and a man,
their household, and their homeland one.
These too, though known, cannot be told
to those who do not know them, and fewer
of us learn them, year by year,
loves that are leaving the world
like the colors of extinct birds,
like the songs of a dead language.

Think of the genius of the animals,
every one truly what it is:
gnat, fox, minnow, swallow, each made
of light and luminous within itself.
They know (better than we do) how
to live in the places where they live.
And so I would like to be a true
human being, dear reader—a choice
not altogether possible now.
But this is what I'm for, the side
I'm on. And this is what you should
expect of me, as I expect it of myself,
though for realization we may wait
a thousand or a million years.

❁❁❁❁❁❁❁

LYSIMACHIA NUMMULARIA

It is called moneywort
for its "coinlike" leaves
and perhaps its golden flowers.
I love it because it is
a naturalized exotic
that does no harm,
and for its lowly thriving,
and for its actual
unlikeness to money.

LEAVINGS

(2010)

I dedicate this book
with respect
to the poet John Haines

LIKE SNOW

Suppose we did our work
like the snow, quietly, quietly,
leaving nothing out.

❀❀❀❀❀❀

ON THE THEORY OF THE BIG BANG
AS THE ORIGIN OF THE UNIVERSE

I.

What banged?

II.

Before banging
how did it get there?

III.

When it got there
where was it?

LOOK IT OVER

I leave behind even
my walking stick. My knife
is in my pocket, but that
I have forgot. I bring
no car, no cell phone,
no computer, no camera,
no CD player, no fax, no
TV, not even a book. I go
into the woods. I sit on
a log provided at no cost.
It is the earth I've come to,
the earth itself, sadly
abused by the stupidity
only humans are capable of
but, as ever, itself. Free.
A bargain! Get it while it lasts.

A LETTER

(to Ed McClanahan)

Dear Ed,
I dreamed that you and I were sent to Hell.
The place we went to was not fiery
or cold, was not Dante's Hell or Milton's,
but was, even so, as true a Hell as any.
It was a place unalterably public
in which crowds of people were rushing
in weary frenzy this way and that,
as when classes change in a university
or at quitting time in a city street,
except that this place was wider far
than we could see, and the crowd as large
as the place. In that crowd every one
was alone. Every one was hurrying.
Nobody was sitting down. Nobody
was standing around. All were rushing
so uniformly in every direction, so
uniformly frantic, that to average them
would have stood them still. It was a place
deeply disturbed. We thought, you and I,
that we might get across and come out
on the other side, if we stayed together,
only if we stayed together. The other side
would be a clear day in a place we would know.
We joined hands and hurried along,
snatching each other through small openings
in the throng. But the place was full
of dire distractions, dire satisfactions.
We were torn apart, and I found you
breakfasting upon a huge fried egg.
I snatched you away: "Ed! Come on!"
And then, still susceptible, I met

369

a lady whose luster no hell could dim.
She took all my thought. But then,
in the midst of my delight, my fear
returned: "Oh! Damn it all! Where's Ed?"
I fled, searching, and found you again.
We went on together. How this ended
I do not know. I woke before it could end.
But, old friend, I want to tell you
how fine it was, what a durable
nucleus of joy it gave my fright
to force that horrid way with you, how
heavenly, let us say, in spite of Hell.

P.S.
Do you want to know why
you were distracted by an egg, and I
by a beautiful lady? That's Hell.

A LETTER

(to my brother)

Dear John,
You said, "Treat your worst enemies
as if they could become your best friends."
You were not the first to perpetrate
such an outrage, but you were right.
Try as we might, we cannot
unspring that trap. We can either
befriend our enemies or we can die
with them, in the absolute triumph
of the absolute horror constructed
by us to save us from them.
Tough, but "All right," our Mary said,
"we'll be nice to the sons of bitches."

A LETTER

(to Hayden Carruth)

Dear Hayden,
How good — how liberating! — to read
of your hatred of *Alice in Wonderland*.
I used to hear my mother reading it
to my sisters, and I hated it too,
but have always been embarrassed
to say so, believing that everybody else
loved it. But who the hell wants to go
down a rabbit hole? I like my feet best
when they're walking on top of the ground.
If I could burrow like a mole, I would,
and I would like that. I would like
to fly like a bird, if I could. Otherwise,
my stratum of choice is the surface.
I prefer skin to anatomy, green grass
to buried rocks, terra firma to the view
from anywhere higher than a tree.
"Long live superficiality!" say I,
as one foot fares waywardly graveward.

A LETTER

(to Ernest J. Gaines)

Dear Ernie,
I've known you since we were scarcely
more than boys, sitting as guests
at Wallace Stegner's table, and I have read
everything you have written since then
because I think what you have written
is beautiful and quietly, steadily
brave, in the manner of the best bravery.
I feel in a way closer to your work
than to that of anybody else of our age.
And why is that? I think it's because
we both knew the talk of old people,
old country people, in summer evenings.
Having worked hard all their lives long
and all the long day, they came out
on the gallery down in your country,
out on the porch or doorstep in mine,
where they would sit at ease in the cool
of evening, and they would talk quietly
of what they had known, of what
they knew. In their rest and quiet talk
there was peace that was almost heavenly,
peace never to be forgotten, never
again quite to be imagined, but peace
above all else that we have longed for.

GIVE IT TIME

The river is of the earth
and it is free. It is rigorously
embanked and bound,
and yet is free. "To hell
with restraint," it says.
"I have got to be going."
It will grind out its dams.
It will go over or around them.
They will become pieces.

QUESTIONNAIRE

1. How much poison are you willing
   to eat for the success of the free
   market and global trade? Please
   name your preferred poisons.

2. For the sake of goodness, how much
   evil are you willing to do?
   Fill in the following blanks
   with the names of your favorite
   evils and acts of hatred.

3. What sacrifices are you prepared
   to make for culture and civilization?
   Please list the monuments, shrines,
   and works of art you would
   most willingly destroy.

4. In the name of patriotism and
   the flag, how much of our beloved
   land are you willing to desecrate?
   List in the following spaces
   the mountains, rivers, towns, farms
   you could most readily do without.

5. State briefly the ideas, ideals, or hopes,
   the energy sources, the kinds of security,
   for which you would kill a child.
   Name, please, the children whom
   you would be willing to kill.

AND I BEG YOUR PARDON

The first mosquito:
come here, and I will kill thee,
holy though thou art.

✿❦✿❦✿❦✿❦✿❦

DAVID JONES

As the soldier takes bodily form
(or dissolves) within the rubble and wreck
of war, so the holy Virgin takes
shape within the world of creatures,
and the angel, to come to her at all,
must wear a caul of birds,
his robe folded like the hills.

✿❦✿❦✿❦✿❦✿❦

TU FU

As I sit here
in my little boat
tied to the shore
of the passing river
in a time of ruin,
I think of you,
old ancestor,
and wish you well.

A SPEECH TO THE GARDEN
CLUB OF AMERICA

With thanks to Wes Jackson and in memory
of Sir Albert Howard and Stan Rowe

Thank you. I'm glad to know we're friends, of course;
There are so many outcomes that are worse.
But I must add I'm sorry for getting here
By a sustained explosion through the air,
Burning the world in fact to rise much higher
Than we should go. The world may end in fire
As prophesied—*our* world! We speak of it
As "fuel" while we burn it in our fit
Of temporary progress, digging up
An antique dark-held luster to corrupt
The present light with smokes and smudges, poison
To outlast time and shatter comprehension.
Burning the world to live in it is wrong,
As wrong as to make war to get along
And be at peace, to falsify the land
By sciences of greed, or by demand
For food that's fast or cheap to falsify
The body's health and pleasure—don't ask why.
But why not play it cool? Why not survive
By Nature's laws that still keep us alive?
Let us enlighten, then, our earthly burdens
By going back to school, this time in gardens
That burn no hotter than the summer day.
By birth and growth, ripeness, death and decay,
By goods that bind us to all living things,
Life of our life, the garden lives and sings.
The Wheel of Life, delight, the fact of wonder,
Contemporary light, work, sweat, and hunger
Bring food to table, food to cellar shelves.
A creature of the surface, like ourselves,
The garden lives by the immortal Wheel

That turns in place, year after year, to heal
It whole. Unlike our economic pyre
That draws from ancient rock a fossil fire,
An anti-life of radiance and fume
That burns as power and remains as doom,
The garden delves no deeper than its roots
And lifts no higher than its leaves and fruits.

WHILE ATTENDING THE ANNUAL
CONVOCATION OF CAUSE THEORISTS
AND BIGBANGISTS AT THE LOCAL PROVINCIAL
RESEARCH UNIVERSITY, THE MAD FARMER
INTERCEDES FROM THE BACK ROW

"Chance" is a poor word among
the mazes of causes and effects, the last
stand of these all-explainers who,
backed up to the first and final Why,
reply, "By chance, of course!" As if
that tied up ignorance with a ribbon.
In the beginning something by chance
existed that would bang and by chance
it banged, obedient to the by-chance
previously existing laws of existence
and banging, from which the rest proceeds
by the logic of cause and effect also
previously existing by chance? Well,
when all that happened who was there?
Did the chance that made the Bang then make
the Bomb, and there was no choice, no help?
Prove to me that chance did ever
make a sycamore tree, a yellow-
throated warbler nesting and singing
high up among the white limbs
and the golden leaf-light, and a man
to love the tree, the bird, the song
his life long, and by his love to save
them, so far, from all machines.
By chance? Prove it, then, and I
by chance will kiss your ass.

MEN UNTRAINED TO COMFORT

Jason Needly found his father, old Ab, at work
at the age of eighty in the topmost
tier of the barn. "Come down!" Jason called.
"You got no business up there at your age."
And his father descended, not by a ladder,
there being none, but by inserting his fingers
into the cracks between boards and climbing
down the wall.

       And when he was young
and some account and strong and knew
nothing of weariness, old man Milt Wright,
back in the days they called him "Steady,"
carried the rastus plow on his shoulder
up the high hill to his tobacco patch, so
when they got there his mule would be fresh,
unsweated, and ready to go.

       Early Rowanberry,
for another, bought a steel-beam breaking plow
at the store in Port William and shouldered it
before the hardly-believing watchers, and carried it
the mile and a half home, down through the woods
along Sand Ripple.

       "But the tiredest my daddy
ever got," his son, Art, told me one day,
"was when he carried fifty rabbits and a big possum
in a sack on his back up onto the point yonder
and out the ridge to town to sell them at the store."

"But why," I asked, "didn't he hitch a team
to the wagon and haul them up there by the road?"

"Well," Art said, "we didn't have but two horses in them days, and we spared them every way we could. A many a time I've seen my daddy or grandpa jump off the wagon or sled and take the end of a singletree beside a horse."

OVER THE EDGE

To tell a girl you loved her—my God!—
that was a leap off a cliff, requiring little
sense, sweet as it was. And I have loved

many girls, women too, who by various fancies
of my mind have seemed loveable. But only
with you have I actually tried it: the long labor,

the selfishness, the self-denial, the children
and grandchildren, the garden rows planted
and gathered, the births and deaths of many years.

We boys, when we were young and romantic
and ignorant, new to the mystery and the power,
would wonder late into the night on the cliff's edge:

Was this love real? Was it true? And how
would you know? Well, it was time would tell,
if you were patient and could spare the time,

a long time, a lot of trouble, a lot of joy.
This one begins to look—would you say?—real?

Index of Titles and First Lines

(Titles are in roman, *first lines in italics*)

383

384

388

✿✧✿✧✿✧✿✧✿

*On the pages whose numbers are given below
the page end coincides with a stanza break:*

4	152
10	190
24	253
37	259
41–44	317
46–54	340
134	359
145	362
149	380
151	

AUTHOR'S NOTE

Earlier printings of this book contained a number of typographical errors—too many, some of them seriously damaging the poems. Because I excused myself from reading the book in proof, those belonged to me, and I apologize for them. I have corrected them for this printing, and in the process, according to habit, I have made perhaps half a dozen small improvements.